I Love America!

A Treasury of Popular Stories, History, Poems, and Songs

Shelagh Canning,
Contributing Editor

A GOLDEN BOOK · NEW YORK
Western Publishing Company, Inc., Racine, Wisconsin 53404

ACKNOWLEDGMENTS

The editor and publisher have made every effort to trace the ownership of all copyrighted material and to secure permission from copyright holders. Any error or omissions are inadvertent, and the publisher will be pleased to make the necessary corrections in future printings. Thanks to the following authors, publishers, and agents for permission to use the material indicated:

Branden Publishing Co., Boston, MA U.S.A., for "The Painted Hills of Arizona," by Edwin Curran.

Brandt & Brandt Literary Agents, Inc., for excerpts from "Benjamin Franklin," by Rosemary and Stephen Vincent Benét. Copyright 1933 by Stephen Vincent Benét. Copyright renewed 1961 by Rosemary Benét.

Curtis Brown, Ltd., for excerpts of "An Introduction to Dogs," from *I'm a Stranger Here Myself*, by Ogden Nash. Copyright 1935 by Ogden Nash.

Jonathan Cape Ltd., for "The Runaway" and "The Road Not Taken," from *The Poetry of Robert Frost*, edited by Edward Connery Lathem.

Robert Frost, The Estate of, for "The Runaway" and "The Road Not Taken," from *The Poetry of Robert Frost*, edited by Edward Connery Lathem.

Harcourt Brace Jovanovich, Inc., for " 'Peculiarsome' Abe," from *Abe Lincoln Grows Up*, by Carl Sandburg. Copyright 1928, 1926 by Harcourt Brace Jovanovich, Inc., and renewed 1956, 1954, 1953 by Carl Sandburg, reprinted by permission of the publisher.

Harcourt Brace Jovanovich, Inc., for excerpts of "Chicago," from *Chicago Poems*, copyright 1916 by Holt, Rinehart and Winston, Inc., and renewed 1944 by Carl Sandburg, reprinted by permission of Harcourt Brace Jovanovich, Inc.

Rosalie Moore Brown, for excerpts from "Catalogue," by Rosalie Moore. Reprinted by permission. © 1940, 1968. Originally in *The New Yorker*.

Harper & Row Jr. Books, for excerpts adapted from "The One Bad Thing About Father," by F. N. Monjo, illustrated by Rocco Negri. Text copyright © 1970 by F. N. Monjo. Pictures copyright © 1970 by Rocco Negri.

Henry Holt and Company, Inc., for "The Runaway" and "The Road Not Taken," from *The Poetry of Robert Frost*, edited by Edward Connery Lathem. Copyright 1916, 1923, © 1969 by Holt, Rinehart and Winston. Copyright 1944, 1951 by Robert Frost. Reprinted by arrangement with Henry Holt and Company, Inc.

Alfred A. Knopf, Inc., for "Aunt Sue's Stories," from *Selected Poems of Langston Hughes*, by Langston Hughes. Copyright 1926 by Alfred A. Knopf, Inc. and renewed 1954 by Langston Hughes. Reprinted by permission of the publisher.

Ellis Lucia, for an excerpt from *The Town That Insulted a President*. Reprinted by permission of the author. All rights reserved.

Little, Brown and Company, for excerpts from "An Introduction to Dogs," from *Family Reunion*, by Ogden Nash. Copyright 1936, 1938, 1950 by Ogden Nash.

Macmillan Publishing Company, for excerpts from *Theodore Roosevelt's Letters to His Children*, edited by Joseph Bucklin Bishop. Reprinted with permission of Charles Scribner's Sons, an imprint of Macmillan Publishing Company. Copyright 1919 Charles Scribner's Sons. Copyright renewed 1947 Edith K. Carow Roosevelt.

Jacob Raeder Marcus, for an excerpt from *Memoirs of American Jews, 1775–1865*. Reprinted by permission of the author. All rights reserved.

Simon & Schuster, for excerpts from *Webster's New World Young Readers' Dictionary* © 1989, 1983, 1979.

Vanguard Press, for "Gray Moss on Green Trees," from *Folk Stories of the South*, by M. A. Jagendorf. Copyright © 1972, 1973 by Vanguard Press, a division of Random House, Inc.

All of the artwork for this book has been specially commissioned from the following artists:

Rose Mary Berlin: Pages 12, 30–31, 92–93
Gene Biggs: Pages 32–36
Jean Chandler: Pages 27, 46, 74–76
Tony Chen: Pages 52–56
Joseph Forte: Pages 15–17, 20–21, 23, 77, 80–81, 88–89
Joy Friedman: Pages 24–25, 57, 59–60, 90
John Gampert: Pages 7, 28–29, 38–41, 85–87, 91
Michael Hampshire: Cover, pages 64–71
Laurie Jordan: Pages 6, 61, 82–84
Kathy Mitchell: Pages 8, 13–14, 50–51, 94
Earl Parker: Endsheets
Jerry Smath: Pages 9–11, 72–73, 79
Richard Walz: Pages 18–19, 62–63

Table of Contents

America

Words by Samuel Francis Smith

With dignity

Music from an old English tune

Columbus

from the poem by Joaquin Miller

Behind him lay the gray Azores,
   Behind the Gates of Hercules;
Before him not the ghost of shores,
   Before him only shoreless seas.
The good mate said: "Now must we pray,
   For lo! the very stars are gone.
Brave Admiral, speak, what shall I say?"
   "Why, say 'Sail on! sail on! and on!'"

"My men grow mutinous day by day;
   My men grow ghastly wan and weak."
The stout mate thought of home; a spray
   Of salt wave washed his swarthy cheek.
"What shall I say, brave Admiral, say,
   If we sight naught but seas at dawn?"
"Why, you shall say at break of day,
   'Sail on! sail on! sail on! and on!'"

Then, pale and worn, he kept his deck,
   And peered through darkness. Ah, that night
Of all dark nights! And then a speck—
   A light! a light! a light! a light!
It grew, a starlit flag unfurled!
   It grew to be Time's burst of dawn.
He gained a world; he gave that world
   Its grandest lesson: "On! sail on!"

Pocahontas

by William Makepeace Thackeray

Wearied arm and broken sword
　　Wage in vain the desperate fight;
Round him press a countless horde,
　　He is but a single knight.
Hark! a cry of triumph shrill
　　Through the wilderness resounds,
　　As, with twenty bleeding wounds,
Sinks the warrior, fighting still.

Now they heap the funeral pyre,
　　And the torch of death they light;
Ah! 'tis hard to die by the fire!
　　Who will shield the captive knight?
Round the stake with fiendish cry
　　Wheel and dance the savage crowd,
　　Cold the victim's mien and proud,
And his breast is bared to die.

Who will shield the fearless heart?
　　Who avert the murderous blade?
From the throng with sudden start
　　See, there springs an Indian maid.
Quick she stands before the knight;
　　"Loose the chain, unbind the ring!
　　I am the daughter of the king,
And I claim the Indian right!"

Dauntlessly aside she flings
　　Lifted axe and thirsty knife,
Fondly to his heart she clings,
　　And her bosom guards his life!
In the woods of Powhatan,
　　Still 't is told by Indian fires
　　How a daughter of their sires
Saved a captive Englishman.

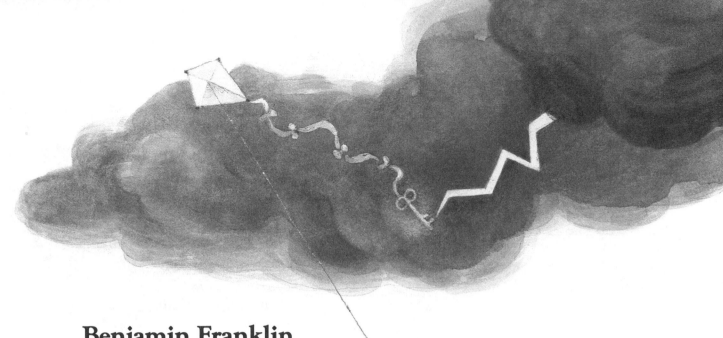

Benjamin Franklin
1706-1790
from the poem by
Rosemary Carr and Stephen Vincent Benét

Ben Franklin munched a loaf of bread
    while walking down the street
And all the Philadelphia girls tee-heed
    to see him eat,
A country boy come up to town with eyes
    as big as saucers
At the ladies in their furbelows, the
    gempmum on their horses.

Ben Franklin wrote an almanac, a smile
    upon his lip,
It told you when to plant your corn and
    how to cure the pip,
But he salted it and seasoned it with proverbs
    sly and sage,
And people read "Poor Richard" till Poor
    Richard was the rage.

Ben Franklin made a pretty kite and flew
    it in the air
To call upon a thunderstorm that happened
    to be there,
—And all our humming dynamos and
    our electric light
Go back to what Ben Franklin found the day
    he flew his kite.

Poor Richard's Almanack

by Benjamin Franklin

Being the choicest Morsels of Wisdom written during the Years of the Almanack's Publication. By that well-known Savant, Dr. Benjamin Franklin of Philadelphia.

Courteous Reader:
It is hardly Necessary to state, that Franklin did not originate all Sayings of Poor Richard. He himself tells us, that they were the "Wisdom of many Ages and Nations..." but with few Exceptions, these Maxims and Aphorisms had been filter'd through Franklin's Brain, and were tinged with that Mother Wit, which so strongly and individually marks so Much that he said and wrote.
—Paul Leichester Ford.

To err is human, to repent divine; to persist devilish.

The Cat in the Gloves catches no Mice.

They who have nothing to trouble them, will be troubled at nothing.

Keep Conscience clear, then never fear.

He that would live in peace and at ease, must not speak all he knows, nor judge all he sees.

The worst wheel of the cart makes the most noise.

Be slow in chusing a friend, slower in changing.

How many observe Christ's Birth-day; How few his Precepts! O, 'tis easier to keep his Holidays than Commandments.

Have you somewhat to do to-morrow, do it today.

Old Boys have their Playthings as well as young Ones; the Difference is only in the Price.

Who has deceiv'd thee so oft as thyself?

Better slip with Foot, than Tongue.

People who are wrapped up in themselves make small packages.

Time lost is never found again.

Haste makes Waste.

'Tis a Shame that your Family is an Honour to you!
You ought to be an Honour to your Family.

Glass, China, and Reputation, are easily crack'd
and never well mended.

He that scatters thorns, let him not go barefoot.

God helps them that help themselves.

Be civil to all; sociable to many; familiar with few;
Friend to one; Enemy to none.

The doors of Wisdom are never shut.

Think of three things—whence you came, where you
are going, and to Whom you must account.

If man could have Half his Wishes, he would
double his Troubles.

An open foe may prove a curse; but a pretended
friend is worse.

Wealth is not his that has it, but his that enjoys it.

Quarrels never could last long, if on one side
only lay the wrong.

Make haste slowly.

Observe all men; thyself most.

Wink at small faults, remember thou has great ones.

A true friend is the best Possession.

A lie stands on one leg, truth on two.

Three may keep a secret if two of them are dead.

11

Yankee Doodle

Words and tune traditional

Arranged by Norman Lloyd

Make it snappy

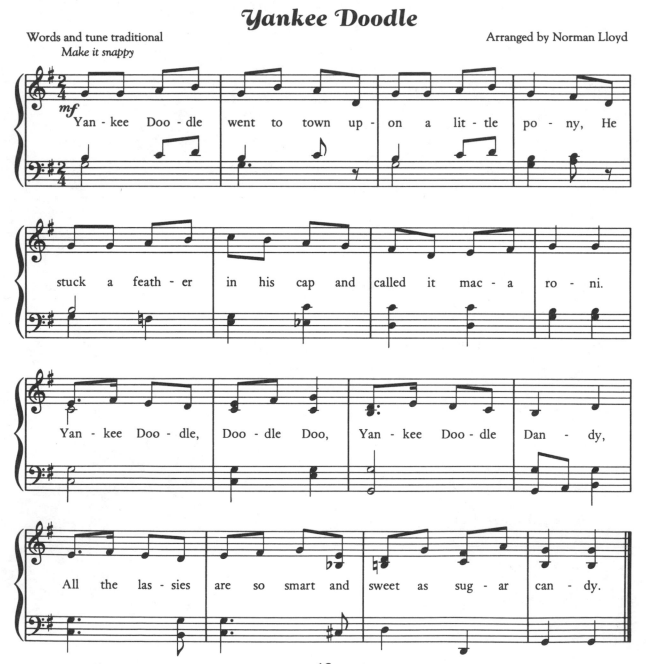

mf Yan - kee Doo - dle went to town up - on a lit - tle po - ny, He
stuck a feath - er in his cap and called it mac - a - ro - ni.
Yan - kee Doo - dle, Doo - dle Doo, Yan - kee Doo - dle Dan - dy,
All the las - sies are so smart and sweet as sug - ar can - dy.

*In the spring of 1775 British General Gage resolved to
make an example of the American patriots Samuel Adams and
John Hancock by arresting them and sending them to England,
where they would be tried for treason. He learned they were in
Lexington, Massachusetts, and decided to trap them. The scheme
was kept under cover; but Paul Revere got wind of it, realized
what was involved, and determined to spread the alarm and
rouse the countryside.*

Paul Revere's Ride

from the poem by
Henry Wadsworth Longfellow

Listen, my children, and you shall hear
Of the midnight ride of Paul Revere,
On the eighteenth of April, in Seventy-five;
Hardly a man is now alive
Who remembers that famous day and year.

He said to his friend, "If the British march
By land or sea from the town to-night,
Hang a lantern aloft in the belfry arch
Of the North Church tower as a signal light,—
One, if by land, and two, if by sea;
And I on the opposite shore will be
Ready to ride and spread the alarm
Through every Middlesex village and farm,
For the country folk to be up and to arm."

A hurry of hoofs in a village street,
A shape in the moonlight, a bulk in the dark,
And beneath, from the pebbles, in passing,
   a spark
Struck out by a steed flying fearless and fleet:
That was all! And yet, through the gloom
   and the light,
The fate of a nation was riding that night;
And the spark struck out by that steed,
   in his flight
Kindled the land into flame with its heat.
He has left the village and mounted the steep,
And beneath him, tranquil and broad and deep,
Is the Mystic, meeting the ocean tides;

13

And under the alders that skirt its edge,
Now soft on the sand, now loud on the ledge,
Is heard the tramp of his steed as he rides.

It was twelve by the village clock,
When he crossed the bridge into Medford town.
He heard the crowing of the cock,
And the barking of the farmer's dog,
And felt the damp of the river fog,
That rises after the sun goes down.
It was one by the village clock,
When he galloped into Lexington.
He saw the gilded weathercock
Swim in the moonlight as he passed.
And the meeting-house windows, blank and bare,
Gaze at him with a spectral glare,
As if they already stood aghast
At the bloody work they would look upon.

You know the rest. In the books you have read,
How the British Regulars fired and fled,—
How the farmers gave them ball for ball,
From behind each fence and farmyard wall,
Chasing the red-coats down the lane,
Then crossing the fields to emerge again
Under the trees at the turn of the road,
And only pausing to fire and load.

So through the night rode Paul Revere,
And so through the night went his cry of alarm
To every Middlesex village and farm,—
A cry of defiance, and not of fear,
A voice in the darkness, a knock at the door,
And a word that shall echo for evermore!
For, borne on the night-wind of the past,
Through all our history, to the last,
In the hour of darkness, and peril, and need,
The people will waken and listen to hear
The hurrying hoof-beats of that steed,
And the midnight message of Paul Revere.

1776—The Declaration of Independence

Soon after the battles of Concord and Lexington, Congress decided to raise an army of 20,000 men. They were called the Continental soldiers, and George Washington was appointed Commander in Chief of all military forces, which now consisted of the Continental soldiers and the militia. Not everyone was in agreement with this turn of events. Many of the colonists hoped for reconciliation with Great Britain and did not relish a seemingly inevitable war. They saw themselves as ill-equipped to take on the world's greatest empire.

However, in January 1776 a pamphlet appeared called *Common Sense*, written by Thomas Paine. Paine strongly supported independence. 'Tis time to part," he said. "The sun never shined on a cause of greater worth. 'Tis not the affair of a city, a county, a province, or a kingdom; but of a continent—at least one-eighth part of the habitable globe." *Common Sense* was a sensation—read by everyone—and the enthusiasm it created soon spread to Congress. The members set up a committee of five—Thomas Jefferson, John Adams, Benjamin Franklin, Roger Sherman, and Robert Livingston—to prepare a declaration of independence. The committee turned over its actual writing to Jefferson, the tall gentleman from Virginia, who they felt was the best writer among them. He was only thirty-three at the time, but his views were well known. He believed it was better "to die free men rather than to live as slaves."

It took Jefferson eighteen days to write the Declaration of Independence. Later, he recalled that he had written it "without reference to book or pamphlet." He did not think it was his duty to "invent new ideas." "The Declaration," he said, "was intended to be an expression of the American mind."

On July 2 the vote for independence was announced and Jefferson presented the Declaration to the Congressional Committee of the Whole. Several days were taken in discussing and changing some of the phrases. In fact, the Congress actually shortened Jefferson's original work. It was signed on July 4 and proclaimed on July 8 in the square outside the Philadelphia State House.

Post riders carried the Declaration to the people. They cheered when they heard the immortal words:

When in the Course of human events, it becomes necessary for one people to dissolve the political bands which have connected them with another, and to assume among the Powers of the earth, the separate and equal station to which the Laws of Nature and of Nature's God entitle them, a decent respect to the opinions of mankind requires that they should declare the causes which impel them to the separation.

We hold these truths to be self-evident, that all men are created equal, that they are endowed by their Creator with certain unalienable Rights, that among these are Life, Liberty and the pursuit of Happiness. That to secure these rights, Governments are instituted among Men, deriving their just powers from the consent of the governed. That whenever any Form of Government becomes destructive of these ends, it is the Right of the People to alter or to abolish it, and to institute new Government, laying its foundation on such principles and organizing its powers in such form, as to them shall seem most likely to effect their Safety and Happiness....

The first of the great truths listed in the Declaration is "that all men are created equal..." They are equal before God and equal before the law. Jefferson and the other delegates knew that the slaves were not treated as equals, but the fact that some men were being denied equality did not change the great truth. Congress was saying, in effect, that all men had the right to be recognized and treated as equals. Congress was setting up a goal, pointing the way toward a more perfect form of society.

Another of the great truths set forth is that God gave all men certain rights which cannot be taken from them; and that among these rights are life, liberty, and the chance to search for happiness.

The Declaration states that people organize governments to protect these rights, and that such governments receive their power from the people themselves. Whenever a government fails to protect these rights the people can make changes in the government, or do away with it, and set up some other form of government to provide for their safety and happiness.

The Declaration then continues with a long list of complaints against the king, showing how his government failed to protect the rights of the American people. The list was intended to prove that King George III "is unfit to be the ruler of a free people."

Now at last Americans knew exactly what they were fighting for: independence, the natural rights of man, and the kind of self-government under which all men could be free and equal.

Ballad of Johnny Appleseed

by Helmer O. Oleson

Through the Appalachian valleys,
   with his kit a buckskin bag,
Johnny Appleseed went plodding past
   high peak and mountain crag.
Oh, his stockings were of leather,
   and his moccasins were tough;
He was set upon a journey where
   the going would be rough.
     See him coming in the springtime,
     Passing violets in the glade.
     Many apple trees are needed,
     And the pioneers want shade.

Johnny carried many orchards in the bag
   upon his back,
And the scent of apple blossoms always
   lingered in his track.
Over half of a fertile continent he planted
   shiny seed;
He would toss them in the clearings where
   the fawn and yearling feed.
     In the summer see him tramping
     Through the windings of the wood.
     Big red apples in the oven
     Make the venison taste good.

18

He would wander over mountain;
    he would brave a raging stream,
For his eyes were filled with visions like
    an ancient prophet's dream.
He would travel after nightfall,
    start again at early morn;
He was planting seeds of apples for the
    children yet unborn.
        Where the autumn leaves turned crimson,
        He was eager to explore.
        Apple dumplings never blossomed
        On a shady sycamore.

Johnny traveled where the war whoop
    of the painted tribes rang loud;
And he walked among grim chieftains
    and their hot-eyed warrior crowd.
He told them of his vision, of his dream
    that would not die,
So he never was molested, and the settlers
    had their pie.
        Bitter winter found him trudging,
        Not for glory or applause,
        Only happy for the winesaps
        In tomorrow's applesauce!

The Star-Spangled Banner

Words by Francis Scott Key

Music by John Stanford Smith

With spirit, not too slow

O—— say, can you see, by the dawn's ear - ly light, What so

proud - ly we hailed, at the twi - light's last gleam - ing? Whose broad stripes and bright

stars, through the per - i - lous fight, O'er the ram - parts we watched, were so

gal - lant - ly stream - ing? And the rock - et's red glare, the bombs

The Flag

On June 14, 1777, at Philadelphia, the Marine Committee of the Second Continental Congress offered the resolution which resulted in the adoption of The Flag of the United States. As new states were admitted it became evident that the number of stripes in the flag would have to be limited. Congress ordered that after July 4, 1818, the flag should have thirteen stripes, symbolizing the thirteen original states, that the union would have twenty stars, and that a new star should be added on the July 4 following admission of a new state. The permanent arrangement of the stars is not designated, and no star is specifically identified with any state. Since 1912, following the admission of a new state, the new design has been announced by executive order. The original resolution read:

> "**Resolved:** that the flag of the United States be made of thirteen stripes, alternate red and white; that the union be thirteen stars, white in a blue field, representing a new constellation."

Pledge of Allegiance

The original version of the Pledge of Allegiance was first published in the September 8, 1892, issue of Youth's Companion, a weekly magazine then published in Boston. The phrase "my flag" contained in the original pledge was changed thirty years later to "the flag of the United States of America." In 1954 the words "under God" were added by an act of Congress. The current official version of the Pledge of Allegiance is as follows:

> "I pledge allegiance to the flag of the United States of America and to the republic for which it stands, one nation under God, indivisible, with liberty and justice for all."

Statue of Liberty

The Statue of Liberty Enlightening the World stands on Liberty Island in New York harbor facing the ocean. Since 1886 it has stood as a symbol of freedom. It was given by the people of France to the United States to commemorate the centennial of American independence. The colossal statue was designed by Fédéric Auguste Bartholdi.

A poem, written by Emma Lazarus, is engraved on a tablet inside the pedestal.

THE NEW COLOSSUS

"Not like the brazen giant of Greek fame,
 With conquering limbs astride from land to land;
 Here at our sea-washed, sunset gates shall stand
 A mighty woman with a torch, whose flame
 Is the imprisoned lightning, and her name
 Mother of Exiles. From her beacon hand
 Glows world-wide welcome; her mild eyes command
 The air-bridged harbor that twin cities frame.
 'Keep, ancient lands, your storied pomp!' cries she
 With silent lips. 'Give me your tired, your poor,
 Your huddled masses yearning to breathe free,
 The wretched refuse of your teeming shore,
 Send these, the homeless, tempest-tost to me,
 I lift my lamp beside the golden door.'"

The Immigrant—1858

from the diary of Jacob Saul Lanzitt, *Memoirs of American Jews, 1775-1865*
by Jacob Raeder Marcus

September 21 Nine-thirty o'clock. Rockets in the air. Gun fired. Ten-twenty-five o'clock: anchored in the channel. Passengers checked until Wed. 22 at 8 o'clock by customs inspectors.

September 29 I arrived in Chicago. I had myself taken to a German hotel, Hotel Meisner, [run by] a very decent man. Oh, how the blood stopped in my veins, not having spoken a word to anyone during the whole journey! I realized that I lack the English language. However, immediately upon my arrival I agreed with the hotelkeeper on $4 per week.

I could not be very demanding. I am in Americka 3,200 miles from Europe, and in Chicago, too, which is 1,200 miles from New York.

Decem. Lost in the cigar business; lost in the beer business.

Decem. 20. Days go by; still no work. Now I have to take hold of whatever there is. I decided to peddle stationery. And now I have been going around for two weeks already, and there was no day when I made my expenses....

I decided to learn a profession; that is, to learn either to make cigars or to sew on Singer's machine. I decided for the latter and began to learn in earnest. Tuition $3. I will probably have to learn for five or six weeks. However, I can make a living. It is hard work, to be sure, but I am now in America; that means working. By chance I got into a factory after ten days' training, though for small wages.

February 20. Still in the same factory with higher wages. By the end of February our factory closed down. I went around for three weeks without work. My money was partly used up. I bought a machine for $40 and went without eating. Finally I came to a Mr. Amer, where I received $7 a week and stayed one month. Now idle for a few days.

All at once I advertised in the paper and was hired by a lining maker for $9 a week. That was too hard. On May 18 a factory opened on William St. Many machines. I came there as an operator for $7 a week and with God's help, I will be able to stay there for some time.

Fourth July. The most famous day in Americka. Love affairs upon love affairs. Patience.

Sunday, August 14. I bought a Singer's machine and traded in my machine, and Monday, August 15, I entered into partnership with a certain Liwey and, God willing, we will do well.

The Constitution of the United States

In May 1787 a convention of delegates from twelve of the thirteen original states met in Philadelphia to draft the Constitution. Rhode Island failed to send a delegate. The convention was presided over by George Washington and lasted until September 17, 1787. The draft was submitted to all thirteen states and was to become effective when nine states ratified it. On June 21, 1788, New Hampshire became the ninth state to approve the draft, and it went into effect the first Wednesday in March 1789.

PREAMBLE

We the people of the United States, in order to form a more perfect Union, establish justice, insure domestic tranquility, provide for the common defense, promote the general welfare, and secure the blessings of liberty to ourselves and our posterity, do ordain and establish this Constitution for the United States of America.

The Bill of Rights, the first ten amendments to the Constitution (proposed on September 25, 1789), was declared in force December 15, 1791. Following is the First Amendment:

Congress shall make no law respecting an establishment of religion or prohibiting the free exercise thereof; or abridging the freedom of speech, or of the press; or the right of the people peaceably to assemble, and to petition the government for a redress of grievances.

Proclamation of Emancipation

That on the first of January, in the year of our Lord one thousand eight hundred and sixty-three, all persons held as slaves within any State, or designated part of a State, the people whereof shall then be in rebellion against the United States, shall be then, thenceforward, and forever free; and the Executive Government of the United States, including the military and naval authority thereof, will recognize and maintain the freedom of such persons, and will do no act or acts to repress such persons, or any of them, in any efforts they may make for their actual freedom.

Aunt Sue's Stories

by Langston Hughes

Aunt Sue has a head full of stories.
Aunt Sue has a whole heart full of stories.
Summer nights on the front porch
Aunt Sue cuddles a brown-faced child to her bosom
And tells him stories.

Black slaves
Working in the hot sun,
And black slaves
Walking in the dewy night,
And black slaves
Singing sorrow songs on the banks of a mighty river
Mingle themselves softly
In the flow of old Aunt Sue's voice,
Mingle themselves softly
In the dark shadows that cross and recross
Aunt Sue's stories.

And the dark-faced child, listening,
Knows that Aunt Sue's stories are real stories.
He knows that Aunt Sue never got her stories
Out of any book at all,
But that they came
Right out of her own life.

The dark-faced child is quiet
Of a summer night
Listening to Aunt Sue's stories.

"Peculiarsome" Abe

from *Abe Lincoln Grows Up* by Carl Sandburg

The farm boys in their evenings at Jones's store in Gentryville talked about how Abe Lincoln was always reading, digging into books, stretching out flat on his stomach in front of the fireplace, studying till midnight and past midnight, picking a piece of charcoal to write on the fire shovel, shaving off what he wrote and then writing more—till midnight and past midnight. The next thing Abe would be reading books between the plow handles, it seemed to them. And once trying to speak a last word, Dennis Hanks said, "There's suthin' peculiarsome about Abe."

He wanted to learn, to know, to live, to reach out; he wanted to satisfy hungers and thirsts he couldn't tell about, this big boy of the backwoods. And some of what he wanted so much, so deep down, seemed to be in the books. Maybe in books he would find the answers to dark questions pushing around in the pools of his thoughts and the drifts of his mind. He told Dennis and other people, "The things I want to know are in books; my best friend is the man who'll git me a book I ain't read." And sometimes friends answered, "Well, books ain't as plenty as wildcats in these parts o' Indianny."

He kept on saying, "Things I want to know are in books; my best friend is the man who'll git me a book I ain't read." He said that to Pitcher, the lawyer over at Rockport, nearly twenty miles away, one fall afternoon, when he walked from Pigeon Creek to Rockport and borrowed a book from Pitcher.

Then when fodder-pulling time came a few days later, he shucked corn from early daylight till sundown along with his father and Dennis Hanks and John Hanks, but after supper he read the book till midnight, and at noon he hardly knew the taste of his cornbread because he had a book in front of him. It was a hundred little things like these which made Dennis Hanks say there was "suthin' peculiarsome" about Abe.

Probably no other people on Earth are as devoted to their animals as Americans. Pets are family. We make movies and TV shows about them, we sing songs about them, and some of our finest poets have celebrated our pets in verse.

The Runaway
by Robert Frost

Once when the snow of the year was beginning to fall,
We stopped by a mountain pasture to say, "Whose colt?"
A little Morgan had one forefoot on the wall,
The other curled at his breast. He dipped his head
And snorted at us. And then he had to bolt.
We heard the miniature thunder where he fled,
And we saw him, or thought we saw him, dim and grey
Like a shadow against the curtain of falling flakes.
"I think the little fellow's afraid of the snow.
He isn't winter-broken. It isn't play
With the little fellow at all. He's running away.
I doubt if even his mother could tell him, 'Sakes,
It's only weather.' He'd think she didn't know!
Where is his mother? He can't be out alone."
And now he comes again with a clatter of stone,
And mounts the wall again with whited eyes
And all his tail that isn't hair up straight.
He shudders his coat as if to throw off flies.
"Whoever it is that leaves him out so late,
When other creatures have gone to stall and bin,
Ought to be told to come and take him in."

30

Catalogue

from the poem by Rosalie Moore

Cats sleep fat and walk thin.
Cats, when they sleep, slump;
When they wake, pull in—
And where the plump's been
There's skin.
Cats walk thin.

Cats wait in a lump,
Jump in a streak.
Cats, when they jump, are sleek
As a grape slipping its skin—
They have technique.
Oh, cats don't creak.
They sneak.

Cats sleep fat.
They spread comfort beneath them
Like a good mat,
As if they picked the place
And then sat.
You walk around one
As if he were the City Hall
After that.

An Introduction to Dogs

from the poem by Ogden Nash

The dog is man's best friend.
He has a tail on one end.
Up in front he has teeth.
And four legs underneath.

Dogs like to bark.
They like it best after dark.
They not only frighten prowlers away
But also hold the sandman at bay.

Dogs display reluctance and wrath
If you try to give them a bath.
They bury bones in hideaways
And half the time they trot sideaways.

The Prairie Traveler

One of the most popular travel guides of a century and more ago was a manual for westward-bound wagon trains and travelers, The Prairie Traveler, *first published in 1859. A travel guide for that purpose was not a description of the marvels to be seen along the way, but a collection of vital information needed for survival. The sampling reprinted here suggests some of the knowledge needed for overland passage. It was written at the request of the War Department, by Captain Randolph B. Marcy, one of the unsung explorers of the American West.*

MEETING INDIANS

On approaching strangers these people put their horses at full speed, and persons not familiar with their peculiarities and habits might interpret this as an act of hostility; but it is their custom with friends as well as enemies, and should not occasion groundless alarm.

When a party is discovered approaching thus, and are near enough to distinguish signals, all that is necessary in order to ascertain their disposition is to raise the right hand with the palm in front, and gradually push it forward and back several times. They all understand this to be a command to halt, and if they are not hostile it will at once be obeyed.

After they have stopped, the right hand is raised again as before, and slowly moved to the right and left, which signifies "I do not know you. Who are you?" As all the wild tribes have their peculiar pantomimic signals by which they are known, they will then answer the inquiry by giving their signal. If this should not be understood, they may be asked if they are friends by raising both hands grasped in the manner of shaking hands, or by locking the two fore-fingers firmly while the hands are held up. If friendly, they will respond with the same signal; but if enemies, they will probably disregard the command to halt, or give the signal of anger by closing the hand, placing it against the forehead, and turning it back and forth while in that position.

The pantomimic vocabulary is understood by all the Prairie Indians, and when oral communication is impracticable it constitutes the court or general council language of the Plains.

The Pony Express

from *Roughing It* by Mark Twain

In a little while all interest was taken up in stretching our necks and watching for the "pony-rider"—the fleet messenger who sped across the continent from St. Joe to Sacramento, carrying letters nineteen hundred miles in eight days! Think of that for perishable horse and human flesh and blood to do! The pony-rider was usually a little bit of a man, brimful of spirit and endurance. No matter what time of the day or night his watch came, and no matter whether it was winter or summer, raining, snowing, hailing, or sleeting, or whether his "beat" was a level straight road or a crazy trail over mountain crags and precipices, or whether it led through peaceful regions or regions that swarmed with hostile Indians, he must be always ready to leap into the saddle and be off like the wind!

There was no idling-time for a pony-rider on duty. He rode fifty miles without stopping, by daylight, moonlight, starlight, or through the blackness of darkness—just as it happened. He rode a splendid horse that was born for a racer and fed and lodged like a gentleman; kept him at his utmost speed for ten miles, and then, as he came crashing up to the station where stood two men holding fast a fresh, impatient steed, the transfer of rider and mailbag was made in the twinkling of an eye, and away flew the eager pair and were out of sight before the spectator could get hardly the ghost of a look. Both horse and rider went "flying light."

The rider's dress was thin, and fitted close. . . . his pantaloons tucked into his boot-tops like a race-rider. He carried no arms—he carried nothing that was not absolutely necessary, for even the postage on his literary freight was worth *five dollars a letter*. He got but little frivolous correspondence to carry—his bag had business letters in it, mostly. His horse was stripped of all unnecessary weight, too. He wore a little wafer of a racing saddle, and no visible blanket. He wore light shoes, or none at all. The little flat mailpockets strapped under the rider's thighs would each hold about the bulk of a child's primer. They held many and many an important business chapter and newspaper letter, but these were written on paper as airy and thin as gold-leaf, nearly, and thus bulk and weight were economized.

The stage-coach traveled about a hundred to a hundred and twenty-five miles a day (twenty-four hours), the pony-rider about two hundred and fifty. There were about eighty pony-riders in the saddle all the time, night and day, stretching in a long, scattering procession from Missouri to California, forty flying eastward, and forty toward the west, and among them making four hundred gallant horses earn a stirring livelihood and see a deal of scenery every single day in the year.

We had had a consuming desire, from the beginning, to see a pony-rider, but somehow or other all that passed us and all that met us managed to streak by in the night, and so we heard only a whiz and a hail, and the swift phantom of the desert was gone before we could get our heads out of the window. But now we were expecting one along every moment and would see him in broad daylight. Presently the driver exclaims:

"Here he comes!"

Every neck is stretched farther and every eye strained wider. Away across the endless dead level of the prairie a black speck appears against the sky, and it is plain that it moves. Well, I should think so! In a second or two it becomes a horse and rider, rising and falling, rising and falling—sweeping toward us nearer and nearer—growing more and more distinct, more and more sharply defined—nearer and still nearer, and the flutter of the hoofs comes faintly to the ear—another instant a whoop and a hurrah from our upper deck, a wave of the driver's hand, but no reply, and man and horse burst past our excited faces and go swinging away like a belated fragment of a storm!

So sudden is it all and so like a flash of unreal fancy that, but for the flake of white foam left quivering and perishing on a mail sack after the vision had flashed by and disappeared, we might have doubted whether we had seen any actual horse and man at all, maybe.

Home on the Range

Words and tune traditional
Moderato

Arranged by Norman Lloyd

Oh, give me a home, where the buf - fa - lo roam, Where the

deer and the an - te - lope play;___ Where sel - dom is heard a dis -

cour - ag - ing word, And the skies are not cloud - y all day.___

Chorus

Home, home on the range,___ Where the deer and the an - te - lope play;___ Where

sel - dom is heard a dis - cour - ag - ing word, And the skies are not cloud - y all day.___

The Town That Insulted a President

from the story by Ellis Lucia

The big news traveled fast through the rough-and-tumble southern Oregon mining town of Jacksonville. President Rutherford B. Hayes was coming to Jacksonville the following week. So the folks painted the town, hung out the flags, swept the boardwalks, and miners took their first baths since Christmas. There was one problem: where would the President and his party stay? The swank new United States Hotel was hardly ready to open. But Madame Holt agreed to speed things up. Carpenters and painters worked day and night, carpets were laid and draperies were hung, the finest upholstery was installed, and crystal chandeliers danced from the ceiling. The President would bask in Victorian splendor.

There was a good reason for President Hayes' visit. He had heard a lot about rowdy old Jacksonville and wanted to see it for himself. He looked forward to this as one of the highlights of his western tour.

By 1880 the cocky, thriving frontier town had survived the invasion of ten thousand gold-crazy miners, continuous skirmishes with the Rogue River Indians, squabbling between Yankee and Southern sympathizers, a near-starvation winter, several disastrous fires, a scarlet fever epidemic, numerous shootings and hangings, and the usual daily barroom brawls that lent character to the West's mining camps. Jacksonville could therefore take the visit of a President in stride.

Like many of its counterparts, Jacksonville was conceived in the lust for gold that inflamed the Old West.

The gold seekers were so excited that in their mad scramble they built Jacksonville right on top of the bonanza they were seeking. The streets were virtually paths of gold, honeycombed with mining shafts and tunnels. The county courthouse was financed with yellow dust from its own excavations. Two enterprising prisoners, serving a stretch in the calaboose, profited handsomely by sinking a shaft in their cell floor.

The network of mines beneath Jacksonville's streets caused no end of trouble during snow runoffs. Sections of streets would suddenly collapse. Houses would rock off their foundations.

Yet at happier times Jacksonville celebrated anniversaries in roaring fashion. Once frolicking soldiers set off an extra-heavy cannon charge, breaking nearly every window in town.

Tales such as these reached the ears of President Hayes, attracting him to this colorful mining center near the California border.

A sizable crowd of gaping citizens had gathered to greet the Chief Executive. Hayes alighted, to be warmly welcomed by the mayor and other local dignitaries. He said a few brief words to the crowd. Then, stiff, hot, and dusty, the President retired to his newly finished suite, its paint hardly dry.

Later President Hayes and his party toured the town. They saw where gold was first discovered and the frantic diggings of Rich Gulch. He fingered the fine yellow dust of a miner's poke, peered into black mine shafts, and drank from the community well. He met miners, cow hands, gamblers, preachers, dance-hall girls, and perhaps a gun slinger or two. He saw a hanging tree.... That night a gala ball was thrown in his honor. Jacksonville's culture might be limited, but the town was trying to do things right.

Next morning folks gathered again as the President prepared to depart.

Families traveled long distances for this brief look at him. As he made his farewells, Madame Holt pushed forward. She handed Hayes a bill for $120 for the night's lodging.

The President flushed. He was taken by surprise.

"But, my dear madame," Hayes stammered, "I most assuredly do not wish to buy your place."

"Mon Dieu!" the proprietress retorted, throwing up her hands. "You object to my price, monsieur? A genteelman like you? It ees a veree fine room you have. We go to much trouble, much expense. Look at zee wallpaper, zee carpeting, zee furniture..."

Hayes was visibly irritated. There was a strained silence. All eyes were on the President, but there were grins on the bewhiskered faces of the miners. Somewhere during his visit he had lost their respect.

No one stepped forward to pay the President's hotel bill.

Finally Hayes directed an aide to settle with Madame Holt. He climbed stiffly into the coach, riding off without any last farewell.

Some said he acted like a stuffed shirt, formal and aloof. Folks were disappointed in his brief public appearances. He didn't stay long at the ball. And Mrs. Hayes apparently insulted Madame Holt by refusing her wine, a symbol of hospitality to the Frenchwoman. A lot of little things, added up, weren't taken kindly by the friendly frontier community.

The crowd stared after the disappearing coach. There were many guffaws as the miners returned to their diggings, the homesteaders to their farms in the Applegate Valley. It was an incident Jacksonville would never forget.

Presidents of the United States of America

Next to the pictures is the name of each President, dates in office, political party, and the name(s) of his Vice President(s).

1. George Washington   1789-97
Federalist

John Adams

---

2. John Adams   1797-1801
Federalist

Thomas Jefferson

---

3. Thomas Jefferson   1801-09
Democratic Republican

Aaron Burr   George Clinton

---

4. James Madison   1809-17
Democratic Republican

George Clinton   Elbridge Gerry

---

5. James Monroe   1817-25
Democratic Republican

Daniel D. Tompkins

---

6. John Quincy Adams   1825-29
Democratic Republican

John C. Calhoun

---

7. Andrew Jackson   1829-37
Democrat

John C. Calhoun   Martin Van Buren

---

8. Martin Van Buren   1837-41
Democrat

Richard M. Johnson

---

9. William Henry Harrison*   1841
Whig

John Tyler

---

10. John Tyler   1841-45
Whig

11. James K. Polk	1845-49	
Democrat		
George M. Dallas		

12. Zachary Taylor*	1849-50	
Whig		
Millard Fillmore		

13. Millard Fillmore	1850-53	
Whig		

14. Franklin Pierce	1853-57	
Democrat		
William R. King		

15. James Buchanan	1857-61	
Democrat		
John C. Breckinridge		

16. Abraham Lincoln**	1861-65	
Republican		
Hannibal Hamlin	Andrew Johnson	

17. Andrew Johnson	1865-69	
Republican		

18. Ulysses S. Grant	1869-77	
Republican		
Schuyler Colfax	Henry Wilson	

19. Rutherford B. Hayes	1877-81	
Republican		
William A. Wheeler		

20. James A. Garfield**	1881	
Republican		
Chester A. Arthur		

*Died in office   **Assassinated

21. Chester A. Arthur Republican	1881-85
22. Grover Cleveland Democrat Thomas A. Hendricks	1885-89
23. Benjamin Harrison Republican Levi P. Morton	1889-93
24. Grover Cleveland Democrat Adlai E. Stevenson	1893-97
25. William McKinley** Republican Garret A. Hobart Theodore Roosevelt	1897-1901
26. Theodore Roosevelt Republican Charles W. Fairbanks	1901-09
27. William Howard Taft Republican James S. Sherman	1909-13
28. Woodrow Wilson Democrat Thomas R. Marshall	1913-21
29. Warren G. Harding* Republican Calvin Coolidge	1921-23
30. Calvin Coolidge Republican Charles G. Dawes	1923-29

★★★★★★★★★★★★★★★★★★★★★★★★★★★★★

31

32

33

31. Herbert C. Hoover   1929-33
Republican
Charles Curtis

32. Franklin D. Roosevelt*   1933-45
Democrat
       John N. Garner
Henry A. Wallace   Harry S. Truman

33. Harry S. Truman   1945-53
Democrat
Alben W. Barkley

34. Dwight D. Eisenhower   1953-61
Republican
Richard M. Nixon

35. John F. Kennedy**   1961-63
Democrat
Lyndon B. Johnson

36. Lyndon B. Johnson   1963-69
Democrat
Hubert H. Humphrey

37. Richard M. Nixon***   1969-74
Republican
Spiro T. Agnew   Gerald R. Ford

38. Gerald R. Ford   1974-77
Republican
Nelson A. Rockefeller

39. Jimmy Carter   1977-81
Democrat
Walter F. Mondale

40. Ronald W. Reagan   1981-89
Republican
George H. W. Bush

41. George H. W. Bush   1989-
Republican
J. Danforth Quayle

34

35

36

37

38

39

40

41

*Died in office   **Assassinated   ***Resigned

STATE	CAPITAL	FLOWER
Alabama	Montgomery	Camellia
Alaska	Juneau	Forget-me-not
Arizona	Phoenix	Saguaro Cactus
Arkansas	Little Rock	Apple Blossom
California	Sacramento	Golden Poppy
Colorado	Denver	Columbine
Connecticut	Hartford	Mountain Laurel
Delaware	Dover	Peach Blossom
Florida	Tallahassee	Orange Blossom
Georgia	Atlanta	Cherokee Rose
Hawaii	Honolulu	Hibiscus
Idaho	Boise	Lewis Mockorange
Illinois	Springfield	Violet
Indiana	Indianapolis	Peony
Iowa	Des Moines	Wild Rose
Kansas	Topeka	Sunflower
Kentucky	Frankfort	Goldenrod
Louisiana	Baton Rouge	Magnolia Grandiflora
Maine	Augusta	Pine Cone and Tassel
Maryland	Annapolis	Black-eyed Susan
Massachusetts	Boston	Trailing Arbutus (Mayflower)
Michigan	Lansing	Apple Blossom
Minnesota	St. Paul	Lady's Slipper
Mississippi	Jackson	Magnolia
Missouri	Jefferson City	Hawthorn
Montana	Helena	Bitterroot Lewisia
Nebraska	Lincoln	Goldenrod
Nevada	Carson City	Sagebrush
New Hampshire	Concord	Purple Lilac
New Jersey	Trenton	Purple Violet
New Mexico	Santa Fe	Yucca
New York	Albany	Rose
North Carolina	Raleigh	Dogwood
North Dakota	Bismarck	Prairie Rose
Ohio	Columbus	Scarlet Carnation
Oklahoma	Oklahoma City	Mistletoe
Oregon	Salem	Oregon Grape
Pennsylvania	Harrisburg	Mountain Laurel
Rhode Island	Providence	Violet
South Carolina	Columbia	Carolina Jessamine
South Dakota	Pierre	Pasque Flower
Tennessee	Nashville	Iris
Texas	Austin	Bluebonnet
Utah	Salt Lake City	Sego Lily
Vermont	Montpelier	Red Clover
Virginia	Richmond	Dogwood
Washington	Olympia	Coast Rhododendron
West Virginia	Charleston	Rosebay Rhododendron
Wisconsin	Madison	Violet
Wyoming	Cheyenne	Indian Paintbrush

The 50 States

Black-eyed Susan

Mockingbird

Cardinal

Apple Blossom

Violet

Chickadee

Bluebird

Wild Rose

Meadowlark

Pasque Flower

BIRD	MOTTO
Yellowhammer	We Dare Defend Our Rights
Willow Ptarmigan	
Cactus Wren	*Ditat Deus*: God Enriches
Mockingbird	*Regnat Populas*: Let the People Rule
Valley Quail	*Eureka*: I Have Found It
Lark Bunting	*Nil Sine Numine*: Nothing Without Duty
American Robin	*Qui Transtulit, Sustinet*: He Who Transplanted, Sustains
Blue Hen Chicken	Liberty and Independence
Mockingbird	In God We Trust
Brown Thrasher	Wisdom, Justice, Moderation
Nene (Hawaiian Goose)	The Life of the Land Is Perpetuated in Righteousness
Mountain Bluebird	*Esto Perpetua*: Exist Forever
Cardinal	State Sovereignty, National Union
Cardinal	Crossroads of America
Eastern Goldfinch	Our Liberties We Prize and Our Rights We Will Maintain
Western Meadowlark	*Ad Astra per Aspera*: To the Stars Through Difficulties
Cardinal	United We Stand, Divided We Fall
Eastern Brown Pelican	Union, Justice, Confidence
Chickadee	*Dirigo*: I Direct
Oriole	*Fatti Maschii, Parole Femine*: Manly Deeds, Womanly Words and *Scuto Bonae Voluntatis Tuae Coronasti Nos*: The Shield of Thy Goodwill Hast Covered Us
Chickadee	*Ense Petit Placidam Sub Libertate Quietem*: By the Sword We Seek Peace, but Peace Only Under Liberty
Robin	*Si Quaeris Peninsulam Amoenam Circumspice*: If You Seek a Pleasant Peninsula, Look About You
Loon	*L'Etoile du Nord*: Star of the North
Mockingbird	*Virtute et Armis*: By Valor and Arms
Eastern Bluebird	*Salus Populi Suprema Lex Esto*: Welfare of the People Shall Be the Supreme Law
Western Meadowlark	*Oro y Plata*: Gold and Silver
Western Meadowlark	Equality Before the Law
Mountain Bluebird	All for Our Country
Purple Finch	Live Free or Die
Eastern Goldfinch	Liberty and Prosperity
Road Runner	*Crescit Eundo*: It Grows as it Goes
Eastern Bluebird	*Excelsior*: Ever Upward
Cardinal	*Esse Quam Videri*: To Be, Rather Than to Seem
Western Meadowlark	Liberty and Union, Now and Forever, One and Inseparable
Cardinal	With God, All Things Are Possible
Scissortailed Flycatcher	*Labor Omnia Vincit*: Labor Conquers All Things
Western Meadowlark	The Union
Ruffed Grouse	Virtue, Liberty and Independence
Rhode Island Red	Hope
Carolina Wren	*Dum Spiro, Spero*: While I Breathe, I Hope and *Animis Opibusque Parati*: Prepared in Mind and Resources
Ringnecked Pheasant	Under God, the People Rule
Mockingbird	Agriculture, Commerce
Mockingbird	Friendship
California Gull	Industry
Hermit Thrush	Freedom and Unity
Cardinal	*Sic Semper Tyrannis*: Thus Always to Tyrants
Willow Goldfinch	*Al-Ki*: Bye and Bye
Cardinal	*Montani Semper Liberi*: Mountaineers Always Free
Robin	Forward
Meadowlark	*Cedant Arma Togae*: Let Arms Yield to the Gown

47

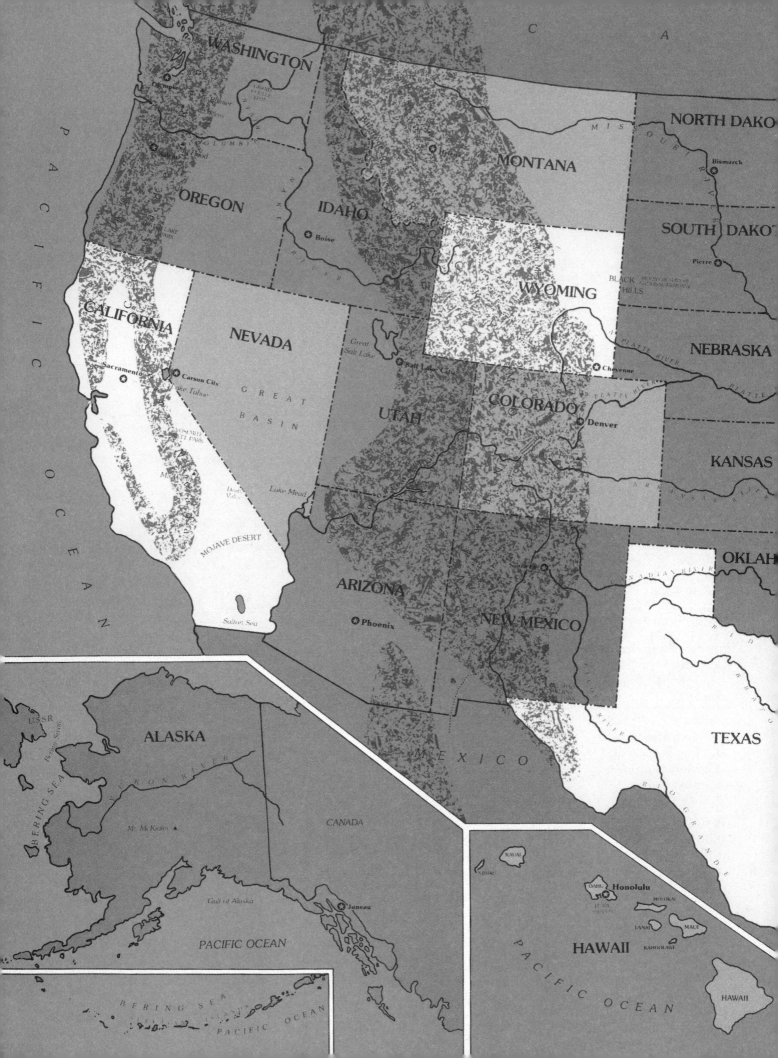

Map of the
UNITED STATES
of America

American poets make us laugh, they make us cry, they fill us with history and romance. They also invite us to look deeper—at faith, at choice, and, best of all, at miracles.

I Never Saw a Moor

by Emily Dickinson

I never saw a moor,
I never saw the sea;
Yet know I how the heather looks,
And what a wave must be.

I never spoke with God,
Nor visited in heaven;
Yet certain am I of the spot
As if the chart were given.

The Road Not Taken

by Robert Frost

Two roads diverged in a yellow wood,
And sorry I could not travel both
And be one traveler, long I stood
And looked down one as far as I could
To where it bent in the undergrowth;

Then took the other, as just as fair,
And having perhaps the better claim,
Because it was grassy and wanted wear;
Though as for that, the passing there
Had worn them really about the same,

And both that morning equally lay
In leaves no step had trodden black.
Oh, I kept the first for another day!
Yet knowing how way leads on to way,
I doubted if I should ever come back.

I shall be telling this with a sigh,
Somewhere ages and ages hence:
Two roads diverged in a wood, and I—
I took the one less traveled by,
And that has made all the difference.

Miracles

by Walt Whitman

Why, who makes much of a miracle?
As to me I know of nothing else but miracles,
Whether I walk the streets of Manhattan,
Or dart my sight over the roofs of houses toward the sky,
Or wade with naked feet along the beach
    just in the edge of the water,
Or stand under trees in the woods,
Or sit at table at dinner with the rest,
Or look at strangers opposite me riding in the car,
Or watch honey-bees busy around the hive
    of a summer forenoon,
Or animals feeding in the fields,
Or birds, or the wonderfulness of insects in the air,
Or the wonderfulness of the sundown,
    or of stars shining so quiet and bright,
Or the exquisite delicate thin curve
    of the new moon in spring;
These with the rest, one and all,
    are to me miracles,
The whole referring, yet each distinct and in its place.

To me every hour of the light and dark is a miracle,
Every cubic inch of space is a miracle,
Every square yard of the surface of the earth
    is spread with the same,
Every foot of the interior swarms with the same.

To me the sea is a continual miracle,
The fishes that swim—the rocks—the motion
    of the waves—the ships with men in them,
What stranger miracles are there?

Little Women

a selection from the book by Louisa May Alcott

*Little Women is the story of the happy, close-knit family life of Marmee
and Father March and their four very special daughters. It is also a story of the
hardships and pain caused by the Civil War and the courage needed to overcome
them. In this chapter, we see that Beth, who was gravely ill with scarlet fever, is
recovering and that Father, who was also dangerously ill, is now well enough to
come home from the war, where he served as a chaplain.*

A CHRISTMAS PRESENT FOR THE MARCH FAMILY

Like sunshine after storm were the peaceful weeks that followed.
Mr. March began to write of returning early in the new year. Beth
improved rapidly and was soon able to lie on the study sofa all day,
amusing herself with the cats and her family of bedraggled dolls. Meg
cooked Beth's favorite dishes, while Amy celebrated her return by giving
away as many of her treasures as her sisters would accept.

The memory of the conversation about Meg and John Brooke weighed
on Jo's spirits. She kept silent, but she watched Meg for "symptoms." "I
caught her singing that song he gave her, and once she said 'John' as you
do," Jo reported gloomily to her mother. "She turned as red as a poppy!
And the other day, when I was looking in her desk for stamps, I found a
bit of paper scribbled over with the words 'Mrs. John Brooke.' Whatever
shall we do?"

"Nothing but wait," her mother answered. "Father's coming will settle
everything. Let's think now about Christmas and make it an especially
happy one."

Several days of unusually fine weather ushered in a splendid Christmas
Day. Beth, wrapped in her mother's gift—a soft, cherry-red dressing
gown—was carried in triumph to the window to behold the offering of Jo
and Laurie. They had made a stately snow maiden in the garden. Crowned
with holly, she bore a basket of fruit in one hand and a great roll of new

music in the other. A bright, woolly afghan was wrapped about her shoulders, and a pink paper streamer held this Christmas carol:

God bless you, Queen Bess!
  May nothing you dismay,
But health and peace and happiness
Be yours, this Christmas Day.

Laurie ran in and out to bring in the gifts, and Jo recited silly speeches as she presented each one.

"I'm so full of happiness," said Beth, "that if Father were only here, I couldn't hold a drop more."

Half an hour later Laurie opened the parlor door and popped his head in. He said very quietly, "Here's another Christmas present for the March family." He might just as well have given an Indian war whoop, for his face and voice gave him away.

Before the words were out of his mouth, a tall man took his place, leaning heavily on the arm of another tall man, who tried to say something and couldn't. There was a general stampede as Mr. March became invisible in the embrace of loving arms. And for the next few minutes, everybody seemed to lose his wits. Jo nearly fainted and had to be comforted on Laurie's shoulder. Mr. Brooke kissed Meg entirely by mistake. Amy tumbled over a stool and, never stopping to get up, hugged her father's boots contentedly.

Suddenly Mrs. March remembered Beth, who had been carried to the next room to rest on the sofa. But joy had put strength into the feeble limbs. The little red wrapper appeared on the threshold, and Beth ran straight into her father's arms.

There never was such a Christmas dinner as they had that day. Mr. Laurence and Laurie dined with them, and also Mr. Brooke—at whom Jo glowered darkly. As twilight gathered, the guests departed, and the happy family sat together around the fire.

"This year has been rather a rough road for you to have traveled, my little pilgrims," Mr. March said. "But you have got on bravely."

"How did you know? Did Mother tell you?" asked Jo.

"A little, and I've made several discoveries today." Mr. March took Meg's hand. "Here's one," he said. "I remember when your first care was to keep your hands white and smooth. They were pretty then, but to me much prettier now, for I read usefulness in these hands."

"What about Jo? Please say something nice," whispered Beth in her father's ear.

"In spite of the curly crop, I don't see the tomboy I left a year ago," said Mr. March. "I rather miss my wild girl, but I have a strong, helpful, tender-hearted woman in her place."

Jo's thin face grew rosy in the firelight as she received her father's praise.

"Now Beth," said Amy, longing for her own turn.

Mr. March just held the little girl close. "I've got you safe, my Beth, and I'll keep you so, please God."

After a minute's silence he looked down at Amy. "I observed that Amy took drumsticks at dinner, though she prefers the breast. I also observe that she does not think so often of her looks, so I conclude that she has learned to think more of other people and less of herself."

"Do you remember," Beth said after a moment, "how after many troubles, Christian and Hopeful came to a pleasant green meadow where they rested before they went on to their journey's end? This is our Pleasant Meadow, isn't it?"

She slipped from her father's arms and went slowly to her little piano and, for the first time in many weeks, touched the keys. As they had always done in times past, the reunited family closed the day with a song.

The Battle Hymn of the Republic
by Julia Ward Howe

Mine eyes have seen the glory of the coming of the Lord:
He is trampling out the vintage where the grapes of wrath are stored;
He hath loosed the fateful lightning of his terrible swift sword:
    This truth is marching on.

Chorus
Glory, glory Hallelujah,
Glory, glory Hallelujah,
Glory, glory Hallclujah,
His truth is marching on.

I have seen him in the watch-fires of a hundred circling camps;
They have builded him an altar in the evening dews and damps;
I can read his righteous sentence by the dim and flaring lamps;
    His day is marching on.

I have read a fiery gospel, writ in burnished rows of steel:
"As ye deal with my contemners, so with you my grace shall deal;
Let the Hero, born of woman, crush the serpent with his heel,
    Since God is marching on."

He has sounded forth the trumpet that shall never call retreat;
He is sifting out the hearts of men before his judgment-seat:
O, be swift, my soul, to answer him! be jubilant, my feet!
    Our god is marching on.

In the beauty of the lilies Christ was born across the sea,
With a glory in his bosom that transfigures you and me;
As he died to make men holy, let us die to make men free,
    While God is marching on.

Dixie

Words and music by Dan Emmett

Arranged by Norman Lloyd

I__ wish I was in the land of cot-ton, Old times there are not for-got-ten, Look a-way! Look a-way! Look a-way! Dix-ie Land. In__ Dix-ie Land where I was born in Ear-ly on one frost-y morn-in', Look a-way! Look a-way! Look a-way! Dix-ie Land.

Chorus

Then I wish I was in Dix-ie, Hoo-ray! Hoo-ray! In Dix-ie Land, I'll take my stand, To live and die in Dix-ie; A-way, A-way, A-way down South in Dix-ie, A-way, A-way, A-way down South in Dix-ie.

Gray Moss on Green Trees

(Choctaw)

The French who came to the New World called the gray tree moss of the South "Spanish beards," and the Spanish called it "French wigs." This is one of many "why" stories that explain it.

The Indians tell a tale down in Louisiana. Maybe it's the Choctaw Indians, maybe it's the Chitimacha Indians, who battled with the French for many years when they were not busy making fine baskets and bright copper things. It might even be another tribe that tells this tale, or it may be all the tribes.

There was an Indian mother working in the field along the river. Near her, her two children played with bows and arrows, and with blue and purple flowers.

Suddenly, cold Wind came racing in the air through the trees. Then Rain came on, sharp rain, running in all directions. Water in the river rose, high and cold.

The mother took the children by the hand and ran toward her hut of palmetto leaves. But she could not run as fast as the flying Wind, or as fast as the racing Water. Water was all around her, coming higher and higher, and held her feet down.

The mother climbed up a thick oak tree, holding the younger child in her arms. The older one followed her slowly. Soon they were high up, where Water could not reach them.

Wind kept on howling and Water kept on rising. Then Rain stopped, but cold Wind still ran wildly in the trees and around the three high up in the branches. The mother and the children were very cold and the children began to cry.

"Mother, my hands are cold and I can't hold on to the branches."

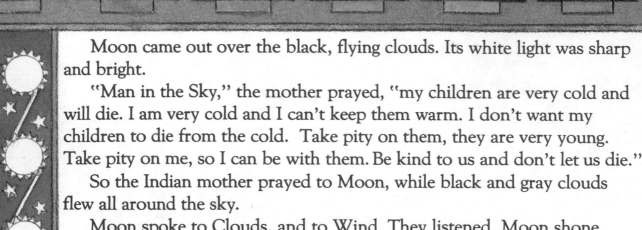

Moon came out over the black, flying clouds. Its white light was sharp and bright.

"Man in the Sky," the mother prayed, "my children are very cold and will die. I am very cold and I can't keep them warm. I don't want my children to die from the cold. Take pity on them, they are very young. Take pity on me, so I can be with them. Be kind to us and don't let us die."

So the Indian mother prayed to Moon, while black and gray clouds flew all around the sky.

Moon spoke to Clouds, and to Wind. They listened. Moon shone strong on the mother and the children, and they fell asleep. Then Moon wove and wove and wove....

Morning came. The sky was clear and warm. The Indian mother and her children awoke and were warm. They looked on the branches and saw what they had never seen before. All over the trees, in the branches and around them, was a thick green-gray blanket that had covered them. It was not made of cloth, but of grass, and Moon had woven it. The Indian mother looked and looked, and so did the children.

"Mother," cried the older boy, "it's a blanket all around us. It kept us warm all night. Moon heard you pray and tore up the clouds to make a blanket for us. Moon hung it on the tree to keep us warm."

"Yes, son, that's what Moon did for us. The sky is clear and the clouds are now on the tree."

They came down and went home.

The "Cloud-Cloth" folks call Spanish moss. It has been on the trees in Louisiana ever since and has spread to trees in other states.

Hiawatha's Childhood

from the poem by Henry Wadsworth Longfellow

Many things Nokomis taught him
Of the stars that shine in heaven;
Showed him Ishkoodah, the comet,
Ishkoodah, with fiery tresses;
Showed the Death-Dance of the spirits,
Warriors with their plumes and war-clubs,
Flaring far away to northward
In the frosty nights of Winter;
Showed the broad, white road in heaven,
Pathway of the ghosts, the shadows,
Running straight across the heavens,
Crowded with the ghosts, the shadows.

At the door on summer evenings
Sat the little Hiawatha;
Heard the whispering of the pine-trees,
Heard the lapping of the water,
Sounds of music, words of wonder;
"Minne-wawa!" said the pine-trees,
"Mudway-aushka!" said the water.

Saw the rainbow in the heaven,
In the eastern sky, the rainbow,
Whispered, "What is that, Nokomis?"

And the good Nokomis answered:
"'T is the heaven of flowers you
see there;
All the wild flowers of the forest,
All the lilies of the prairie,
When on earth they fade and perish,
Blossom in the heaven above us."

Then the little Hiawatha
Learned of every bird its language,
Learned their names and all their secrets,
How they built their nests in Summer,
Where they hid themselves in Winter,
Talked with them whene'er he met them,
Called them "Hiawatha's Chickens."

Of all beasts he learned the language,
Learned their names and all their secrets,
How the beavers built their lodges,
Where the squirrels hid their acorns,
How the reindeer ran so swiftly,
Why the rabbit was so timid,
Talked with them whene'er he met them,
Called them "Hiawatha's Brothers."

Paul Bunyan

The rivers in the great Northland run swift, and the trees grow tall enough to blot out the sun. It took big men to tame that timber, and Paul Bunyan was the biggest and greatest logger of them all. It was said that his cradle was so big, it was anchored in the ocean off the shore. It took a whole town to raise that child, and when Paul saw that he was eating them out of house and home, he went West where there was plenty of room.

Paul had no more than reached the Middle West when the Winter of the Blue Snow came howling down. Yessir, the snow was blue with cold that year.

One day as Paul was snowshoeing over the countryside, he saw a big blue drift shiver and shake. Well, he shoved away the drift, and what should he find but a calf, turned blue from the cold.

That calf was no more than six feet high, so Paul thawed him out and named him Babe and took him home for a pet. But Babe grew two feet every time anyone looked at him! Soon he was quite some size—as big for an ox as Paul was for a man. That was going some! And he stayed bright blue.

When spring came Paul and Babe wandered around the countryside, looking for a job their size. Babe's hoofs sank into the soft spring ground as they went. The spring rains filled the hoofprints and made the lakes you see to this day out in Wisconsin and Minnesota.

Paul took another look around the countryside. "Trees!" he said to Babe. "That's what grows biggest in this ground. Trees are the crop for you and me. We'll set us up a lumber camp, Babe, my friend!"

When Paul needed a meal, he could always do some hunting. There were plenty of bear, deer, moose, and wolves around in those days— though even Paul would admit that wolf meat doesn't make much of a meal. When Paul was hunting, just for fun he liked to straighten out twisting animal trails. He'd fasten Babe's harness to one end and just pull away in a good straight line. You could hear the crunching back in the trees as that old trail straightened out. One of those trails makes the boundary line between the Dakotas today.

Babe was handy in other ways, too. When Paul and his crew got their first forest lumbered off, they found they had forgotten something. There was no river to float the logs down. They were a good long distance from a sawmill and there were no roads between.

That didn't stop Paul for long. He hitched Babe to a plow and they dug them a river, right over to the Mississippi, and the logs went floating down. The Missouri is what folks call that stream Babe and Paul Bunyan dug.

The Glorious Whitewasher

from *The Adventures of Tom Sawyer* by Mark Twain

Saturday morning was come, and all the summer world was bright and fresh, and brimming with life. There was a song in every heart; and if the heart was young the music issued at the lips. There was cheer in every face and a spring in every step. The locust trees were in bloom and the fragrance of the blossoms filled the air. Cardiff Hill, beyond the village and above it, was green with vegetation, and it lay just far enough away to seem a Delectable Land, dreamy, reposeful, and inviting.

Tom appeared on the sidewalk with a bucket of whitewash and a long-handled brush. He surveyed the fence, and all gladness left him and a deep melancholy settled down upon his spirit. Thirty yards of board fence nine feet high. Life to him seemed hollow, and existence but a burden. Sighing he dipped his brush and passed it along the topmost plank; repeated the operation, did it again; compared the insignificant whitewashed streak with the far-reaching continent of unwhitewashed fence, and sat down on a tree-box discouraged.

Jim came skipping out at the gate with a tin pail, and singing "Buffalo Gals." Bringing water from the town pump had always been hateful work in Tom's eyes, before, but now it did not strike him so. He remembered that there was company at the pump. White, mulatto, and Negro boys and girls were always there waiting their turns, resting, trading playthings, quarreling, fighting, skylarking. And he remembered that although the pump was only a hundred and fifty yards off, Jim never got back with a bucket of water under an hour—and even then somebody generally had to go after him. Tom said:

"Say, Jim, I'll fetch the water if you'll whitewash some."

"Can't, Mars Tom. Ole missis, she tole me I got to go an' git dis water an' not stop foolin' roun' wid anybody. She say she spec' Mars Tom gwine to ax me to whitewash, an' so she tole me go 'long an' 'tend to my own business—she 'lowed she'd 'tend to de whitewashin'."

"Oh, never you mind what she said, Jim. That's the way she always talks. Gimme the bucket—I won't be gone only a minute. She won't ever know."

"Oh, I dasn't, Mars Tom. Ole missis she'd take an' tar de head off'n me. 'Deed she would."

"She! She never licks anybody—whacks 'em over the head with her thimble—and who cares for that, I'd like to know. She talks awful, but talk don't hurt—anyways it don't if she don't cry. Jim, I'll give you a marvel. I'll give you a white alley!"

Jim began to waver.

"White alley, Jim! And it's a bully taw."

"My! Dat's a mighty gay marvel, I tell you! But Mars Tom, I's powerful 'fraid ole missis—"

"And besides, if you will I'll show you my sore toe."

Jim was only human—this attraction was too much for him. He put down his pail, took the white alley, and bent over the toe with absorbing interest while the bandage was being unwound. In another moment he was flying down the street with his pail and a tingling rear, Tom was whitewashing with vigor, and Aunt Polly was retiring from the field with a slipper in her hand and triumph in her eye.

But Tom's energy did not last. He began to think of the fun he had
planned for this day, and his sorrows multiplied. Soon the free boys
would come tripping along on all sorts of delicious expeditions, and they
would make a world of fun of him for having to work—the very thought
of it burnt him like fire. He got out his worldly wealth and examined it—
bits of toys, marbles, and trash; enough to buy an exchange of work, maybe,
but not half enough to buy so much as half an hour of pure freedom. So
he returned his straitened means to his pocket, and gave up the idea of
trying to buy the boys. At this dark and hopeless moment an inspiration
burst upon him! Nothing less than a great, magnificent inspiration.

He took up his brush and went tranquilly to work. Ben Rogers hove
in sight presently—the very boy, of all boys, whose ridicule he had been
dreading. Ben's gait was the hop-skip-and-jump—proof enough that his
heart was light and his anticipations high. He was eating an apple, and
giving a long, melodious whoop, at intervals, followed by a deep-toned
ding-dong-dong, ding-dong-dong, for he was personating a steamboat. As
he drew near, he slackened speed, took the middle of the street, leaned far
over the starboard and rounded to ponderously and with laborious pomp
and circumstance—for he was personating the Big Missouri, and considered himself to be drawing nine feet of water. He was boat and captain
and engine-bells combined, so he had to imagine himself standing on his
own hurricane-deck giving the orders and executing them:

"Stop her, sir! Ting-a-ling-ling!" The headway ran almost out and he
drew up slowly toward the sidewalk.

"Ship up to back! Ting-a-ling-ling!" His arms straightened and
stiffened down his sides.

"Set her back on the stabboard! Ting-a-ling-ling! Chow! ch-chow-wow! Chow!" His right hand, meantime, describing stately circles—for it was representing a forty-foot wheel.

"Let her go back to the labboard! Ting-a-ling-ling! Chow-ch-chow-chow!" The left hand began to describe circles.

"Stop the labboard! Come ahead on the stabboard! Stop her! Let your outside turn over slow! Ting-a-ling-ling! Chow-ow-ow! Get out that head-line! Lively now! Come—out with your spring-line—what're you about there! Take a turn round that stump with the bight of it! Stand by that stage, now—let her go! Done with the engines, sir! Ting-a-ling-ling! Sh't! s'h't! sh't!" (trying the gaugecocks).

Tom went on whitewashing—paid no attention to the steamboat. Ben stared a moment and then said:

"Hi-yi! You're up a stump, ain't you!"

No answer. Tom surveyed his last touch with the eye of an artist, then he gave his brush another gentle sweep and surveyed the result, as before. Ben ranged up alongside of him. Tom's mouth watered for the apple, but he stuck to his work. Ben said:

"Hello, old chap, you got to work, hey?"

Tom wheeled suddenly and said:

"Why, it's you, Ben! I warn't noticing."

"Say—I'm going in a-swimming. I am. Don't you wish you could? But of course you'd druther work—wouldn't you? Course you would!"

Tom contemplated the boy a bit, and said:

"What do you call work?"

"Why, ain't that work?"

Tom resumed his whitewashing, and answered carelessly:

"Well, maybe it is, and maybe it ain't. All I know is, it suits Tom Sawyer."

"Oh, come, now, you don't mean to let on that you like it?"

The brush continued to move.

"Like it? Well, I don't see why I oughtn't to like it. Does a boy get a chance to whitewash a fence every day?"

That put the thing in a new light. Ben stopped nibbling his apple. Tom swept his brush daintily back and forth—stepped back to note the effect—added a touch here and there—criticized the effect again—Ben watching every move and getting more and more interested, more and more absorbed. Presently he said:

"Say, Tom, let me whitewash a little."

Tom considered, was about to consent; but he altered his mind:

"No—no—I reckon it wouldn't hardly do, Ben. You see, Aunt Polly's awful particular about this fence—right here on the street, you know—but if it was the back fence I wouldn't mind and she wouldn't. Yes, she's awful particular about this fence; it's got to be done very careful; I reckon there ain't one boy in a thousand, maybe two thousand, that can do it the way it's got to be done."

"No—is that so? Oh, come, now—lemme just try. Only just a little—I'd let you, if you was me, Tom."

"Ben, I'd like to, honest injun; but Aunt Polly—well, Jim wanted to do it, but she wouldn't let him; Sid wanted to do it, and she wouldn't let Sid. Now don't you see how I'm fixed? If you was to tackle this fence and anything was to happen to it—"

"Oh, shucks, I'll be just as careful. Now lemme try. Say—I'll give you the core of my apple."

"Well, here—No, Ben, now don't. I'm afeared—"

"I'll give you all of it!"

Tom gave up the brush with reluctance in his face, but alacrity in his heart. And while the late steamer Big Missouri worked and sweated in the sun, the retired artist sat on a barrel in the shade close by, dangled his legs, munched his apple, and planned the slaughter of more innocents. There was no lack of material; boys happened along every little while; they came to jeer, but remained to whitewash. By the time Ben was fagged out, Tom had traded the next chance to Billy Fisher for a kite, in good repair; and when he played out, Johnny Miller bought in for a dead rat and a string to swing it with—and so on, and so on, hour after hour. And when the middle of the afternoon came, from being a poor poverty-stricken boy in the morning, Tom was literally rolling in wealth. He had beside the things before mentioned, twelve marbles, part of a jews'-harp, a piece of blue bottle-glass to look through, a spool cannon, a key that wouldn't unlock anything, a fragment of chalk, a glass stopper of a

decanter, a tin soldier, a couple of tadpoles, six firecrackers, a kitten with only one eye, a brass door-knob, a dog-collar—but no dog—the handle of a knife, four pieces of orange-peel and a dilapidated old window-sash.

He had had a nice, good, idle time all the while—plenty of company—and the fence had three coats of whitewash on it! If he hadn't run out of whitewash, he would have bankrupted every boy in the village.

Tom said to himself that it was not such a hollow world, after all. He had discovered a great law of human action, without knowing it—namely, that in order to make a man or a boy covet a thing, it is only necessary to make the thing difficult to attain. If he had been a great and wise philosopher, like the writer of this book, he would now have comprehended that Work consists of whatever a body is obliged to do, and that Play consists of whatever a body is not obliged to do. And this would help him to understand why constructing artificial flowers or performing on a treadmill is work, while rolling tenpins or climbing Mont Blanc is only amusement. There are wealthy gentlemen in England who drive four-horse passenger-coaches twenty or thirty miles on a daily line, in the summer, because the privilege costs them considerable money; but if they were offered wages for the service, that would turn it into work and then they would resign.

The boy mused awhile over the substantial change which had taken place in his worldly circumstances, and then wended toward headquarters to report.

Casey at the Bat
by Ernest Lawrence Thayer

The outlook wasn't brilliant for the Mudville nine that day;
The score stood four to two with but one inning more to play.
And then when Cooney died at first, and Barrow did the same,
A sickly silence fell upon the patrons at the game.

A straggling few got up to go in deep despair. The rest
Clung to that hope which springs eternal in the human breast;
They thought if only Casey could but get a whack at that—
We'd put up even money now with Casey at the bat.

But Flynn preceded Casey, as did also Jimmy Blake,
And the former was a lulu and the latter was a cake;
So upon that stricken multitude grim melancholy sat,
For there seemed but little chance of Casey's
getting to the bat.

But Flynn let drive a single, to the wonderment of all,
And Blake, the much despis-ed, tore the cover off the ball;
And when the dust had lifted, and the men saw what had occurred,
There was Jimmy safe at second, and Flynn a-hugging third.

Then from 5,000 throats and more there rose a lusty yell;
It rumbled through the valley, it rattled in the dell;
It knocked upon the mountain and recoiled upon the flat,
For Casey, mighty Casey, was advancing to the bat.

There was ease in Casey's manner as he stepped into his place;
There was pride in Casey's bearing and a smile on Casey's face.
And when, responding to the cheers, he lightly doffed his hat,
No stranger in the crowd could doubt 'twas Casey at the bat.

Ten thousand eyes were on him as he rubbed his hands with dirt;
Five thousand tongues applauded when he wiped them on his shirt.
Then while the writhing pitcher ground the ball into his hip,
Defiance gleamed in Casey's eye, a sneer curled Casey's lip.

And now the leather-covered sphere came hurtling through the air,
And Casey stood a-watching it in haughty grandeur there.
Close by the sturdy batsman the ball unheeded sped—
"That ain't my style," said Casey. "Strike one,"
    the umpire said.

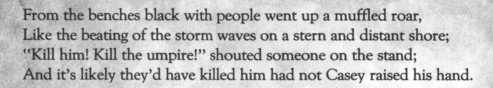

From the benches black with people went up a muffled roar,
Like the beating of the storm waves on a stern and distant shore;
"Kill him! Kill the umpire!" shouted someone on the stand;
And it's likely they'd have killed him had not Casey raised his hand.

With a smile of Christian charity great Casey's visage shone;
He stilled the rising tumult; he bade the game go on;
He signaled to the pitcher, and once more the spheroid flew;
But Casey still ignored it, and the umpire said, "Strike two."

"Fraud!!" cried the maddened thousands, and echo answered "fraud";
But one scornful look from Casey and the audience was awed.
They saw his face grow stern and cold, they saw his muscles strain.
And they knew that Casey wouldn't let that ball go by again.

The sneer is gone from Casey's lip, his teeth are clenched in hate;
He pounds with cruel violence the bat upon the plate.
And now the pitcher holds the ball, and now he lets it go,
And now the air is shattered by the force of Casey's blow.

Oh, somewhere in this favored land the sun is shining bright;
The band is playing somewhere, and somewhere hearts are light;
And somewhere men are laughing, and somewhere children shout;
But there is no joy in Mudville—mighty Casey has struck out.

JERRY SMATH

The Wonderful Tar-Baby Story

from *Uncle Remus, His Songs and Sayings* by Joel Chandler Harris

"Didn't the fox *never* catch the rabbit, Uncle Remus?" the little boy asked the old man one evening.

"He come mighty nigh it, honey, sure as you're born. One day after Brer Rabbit had fooled him so many times, Brer Fox went to work an' got him some tar, an' then he mixed it with some turpentine an' fixed up a contraption that he called a Tar-Baby. He took this here Tar-Baby an' set him down right smack in the big road an' then lay down in the bushes an' watched for to see what was goin' to happen.

"Brer Fox didn't have to wait long either. Pretty soon Brer Rabbit come prancin' down the road lippity-clippity, clippity-lippity, just as sassy as a jay-bird. Brer Fox, he lay low. Brer Rabbit come prancin' right along 'til he spied the Tar-Baby settin' there, an' then he fetched up on his hind legs lookin' mighty astonished. The Tar-Baby just set there doin' nothin', an' Brer Fox, he kept on layin' low.

"'Mornin'!' says Brer Rabbit. 'Nice weather this mornin',' says he.

"Tar-Baby ain't sayin' nothin', an' Brer Fox, he lay low.

"'How is the state of your health at present?' says Brer Rabbit to Tar-Baby.

"Brer Fox, he wing his eye slow, an' lay low, an' Tar-Baby she ain't sayin' nothin'.

"'How you gettin' along?' says Brer Rabbit. An' when there ain't no answer, he says, 'Is you deaf?' He says, 'Because if you is, I can holler louder.'

"Tar-Baby just kept on settin' there, an' Brer Fox he lay low.

"'You're mighty stuck up, that's what you is,' says Brer Rabbit. 'An' I'm goin' to cure you, that's what I'm goin' to do,' he says.

"Brer Fox, he sorta chuckle in his stomach, he did, but Tar-Baby ain't sayin' nothin'.

"'I'm going to learn you how to talk to respectable folk if it's the last

74

thing I do,' says Brer Rabbit. 'If you don't take off that old hat an' say howdy-do to me, I'm going to bust you wide open,' says he.

"Tar-Baby stay still, an' Brer Fox lay low.

"Brer Rabbit kept on askin' him to say howdy-do, an' Tar-Baby kept on sayin' nothin' at all, 'til finally Brer Rabbit draw back his fist and— *blip*—he hit Tar-Baby right smack on the side of the head. Right there's where Brer Rabbit made his big mistake. His fist stuck fast, an' he couldn't pull loose. The tar held him tight. But Tar-Baby just set still. And Brer Fox, he lay low.

"'If you don't let me loose, I'll knock you again,' says Brer Rabbit, an' with that he fetched Tar-Baby a swipe with the other hand. An' *that* stuck. Tar-Baby, she ain't sayin' nothin', and Brer Fox, he lay low.

"'Turn me loose,' hollers Brer Rabbit. 'Turn me loose before I kick the natural stuffin' out of you,' he says. But Tar-Baby ain't sayin' nothin'— just keeps on holdin' fast. Then Brer Rabbit he commenced to kick, an'

the next thing he know his feet are stuck fast, too. Brer Rabbit squall out that if Tar-Baby didn't turn him loose, he'd butt with his head. Brer Rabbit butted, an' then he got his head stuck, too.

"Then Brer Fox, he sauntered out of the bushes, lookin' just as innocent as a mockin'bird.

"'Howdy, Brer Rabbit,' says Brer Fox, says he. 'You look sort of stuck up this mornin',' he says, an' then he rolled on the ground and he laughed and laughed 'til he couldn't laugh no more. 'I reckon you're goin' to have dinner with me this time, Brer Rabbit,' he says. 'I've laid in a heap o' nice vegetables an' things, an' I ain't goin' to take no excuse,' says Brer Fox."

Here Uncle Remus paused and raked a huge sweet potato out of the ashes on the hearth.

"Did the fox eat the rabbit, Uncle Remus?" asked the little boy.

"Well, now, that's as far as the tale goes," replied the old man. "Maybe he did—an' then again, maybe he didn't. Some people say that Judge B'ar come along an' turned him loose. And some say he didn't.... But ain't that Miss Sally I hear callin' you? You better run along now."

The One Bad Thing About Father

from the poem by Ferdinand Monjo

*Ferdinand Monjo, in this invented diary of Theodore Roosevelt's son
Quentin, succeeds in capturing both the robust personality of President
Roosevelt and the somewhat biased viewpoint of his child. On the other hand,
the deep affection Roosevelt felt for his children is captured in his very real
letters that follow this poem.*

ARCHIE AND I
I'm Quentin.
Here's my brother Archie.
And here's Father.
There's just one bad thing about Father.
He's President of the United States.
That means he has to live in the White House.
And all the rest of us—
Mother
Alice
Ted
Kermit
Ethel
Archie
and me—
we all have to live there too.
There's one thing Archie and I
can't understand about Father.
I mean, Father could have been
a boxer or a wrestler.
He can even do jujitsu.
Mother says
he could have headed the police force
in New York City forever if he had wanted to.

Our brother Ted says
Father could have kept on being a cowboy
on his ranch in the West.
Father showed Archie and me his brand
for branding cattle. Here it is:

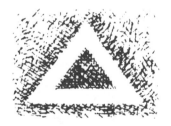

Father could have been a general.
Our sister Alice says
Father was a brave soldier and
helped win a war in Cuba.
And Father could have been a hunter.
Our brother Kermit says
Father knows how to catch
wild cats and bears.
Now if Father can do all these things,
what Archie and I would like to know is
how come he'd rather be President?

T. R. Writes His Son

with his own illustrations

Tenesas Bayou, Oct. 10, 1907.

Blessed Archie:

I just loved your letter. I was so glad to hear from you. I was afraid you would have trouble with your Latin....How do you get on at football?

We have found no bear. I shot a deer; I sent a picture of it to Kermit.

A small boy here caught several wildcats. When one was in the trap he would push a box towards it, and it would itself get into it, to hide; and so he would capture it alive. But one, instead of getting into the box, combed the hair of the small boy!

We have a great many hounds in camp; at night they gaze solemnly into the fire.

Dr. Lambert has caught a good many bass, which we have enjoyed at the camp table.

Bear Bayou, Oct. 16, 1907.

Darling Archie:

We have had no luck with the bear; but we have killed as many deer as we needed for meat, and the hounds caught a wildcat. Our camp is as comfortable as possible, and we have great camp fires at night.

One of the bear-hunting planters with me told me he once saw a bear, when overtaken by the hounds, lie down flat on its back with all its legs stretched out, while the dogs barked furiously all around it.

Suddenly the bear sat up with a jump, and frightened all the dogs so that they nearly turned back somersaults.

At this camp there is a nice tame pussy-cat which lies out here all the time, catching birds, mice, or lizards; but very friendly with any party of hunters which happens along.

The Bear Plays Dead

The Bear Sits Up

Talking American

"English" is the language spoken in **America**. However it certainly has changed in the past 300 years. The colonists did not have English names for many of the new plants and animals they found here, so they picked up words like **skunk** and **moose** from the Indians. They also made up descriptive and fanciful names like **shovel-nosed fish** and **dumb rattlesnake** (for the **copperhead**, because it has *no* **rattles**) and **Dutchman's pipe** for a flowering vine. A brilliantly colored wildflower is called **Indian paintbrush**.

As **settlers** came from other countries around the world, they, too, contributed new words to the language. **Tuna** is from Spanish, **pants** from French, **jumbo** is from Africa, **cookie** is Dutch, **schlepp** Yiddish.

Some things were named for people: **Teddy bear** for **President** Theodore Roosevelt, **sideburns** or **burnsides** for **Civil War** General Ambrose Burnsides, who sported an unusual cut of beard.

Many of the words we use today have changed over the years. For example, **bully** was the class leader at Yale years ago, and a **cowboy** was a Tory guerrilla during the **Revolutionary War.** The Tories would hide in the bushes and lure patriots looking for food into an ambush by tinkling cow bells. Today, of course, **cowboys** are usually found in the **West** and elsewhere on **dude ranches**.

At the turn of the century, fishermen and sailors, as well as ladies, wore **petticoats**. These were very wide trousers that came down to the calf. And if we were to travel back in time, we would be surprised to learn that a **barber** is a cold wind driving snow so violently that some thought it could cut your face.

There are thousands of these **Americanisms**. All you need to find more is a dictionary that features a star before these words and expressions.

America is made up of all kinds of places: big cities and small towns, farmlands and seashores, mountains and valleys. And each of us may find different things as we visit our country. Here are some impressions.

Boston
by John Collins Bossidy

Here's to good old Boston,
    The home of the bean and the cod,
Where the Lowells talk only to Cabots,
    And the Cabots talk only to God.

Chicago
from the poem by Carl Sandburg

Hog Butcher for the World,
Tool Maker, Stacker of Wheat,
Player with Railroads and the Nation's
    Freight Handler;
Stormy, husky, brawling,
City of the Big Shoulders...

Mannahatta
from the poem by Walt Whitman

Numberless crowded streets—high growths of iron,
    slender, strong, light, splendidly uprising
    toward clear skies...
The countless masts, the white shore-steamers,
    the lighters, the ferry-boats, the black sea-steamers
    well-model'd;
The down-town streets, the jobbers' houses of business—
    the houses of business of the ship-merchants,
    and moneybrokers—the river-streets....
Immigrants arriving fifteen or twenty thousand in a week;
The carts hauling goods—the manly race of drivers
    of horses—the brown-faced sailors....
The parades, processions, bugles playing, flags flying,
    drums beating....

80

The Painted Hills of Arizona
by Edwin Curran

The rainbows all lie crumpled on these hills,
The red dawns scattered on their colored sills.
These hills have caught the lightning in its flight,
Caught colors from the skies of day and night
And shine with shattered stars and suns; they hold
Dyed yellow, red and purple, blue and gold.
Red roses seem within their marble blown,
A painted garden chiseled in the stone;
The rose and violet trickling through their veins,
Where they drop brilliant curtains to the plains—
A ramp of rock and granite, jeweled and brightening
Like some great colored wall of sudden lightning!

Boonder

from the story by Bret Harte,
known as the "father of American local color."

I never knew how the subject of this memoir came to attach himself so closely to the affections of my family. He was not a prepossessing dog. He was not a dog of even average birth and breeding. His pedigree was involved in the deepest obscurity. He may have had brothers and sisters, but in the whole range of my canine acquaintance (a pretty extensive one), I never detected any of Boonder's peculiarities in any other of his species. His body was long, and his forelegs and hindlegs were very wide apart, as though Nature originally intended to put an extra pair between them, but had unwisely allowed herself to be persuaded out of it. This peculiarity was annoying on cold nights, as it always prolonged the interval of keeping the door open for Boonder's ingress long enough to allow two or three dogs of a reasonable length to enter. Boonder's feet were decided; his toes turned out considerably, and in repose his favorite attitude was the first position of dancing. Add to a pair of bright eyes ears that seemed to belong to some other dog, and a symmetrically pointed nose that fitted all apertures like a pass-key, and you have Boonder as we knew him.

I am inclined to think that his popularity was mainly owing to his quiet impudence. His advent in the family was that of an old member, who had been absent for a short time, but had returned to familiar haunts and associations. . . . Bone-burying was Boonder's great weakness. He was at first discovered coiled up on a rug in an upper chamber, and was the least disconcerted of the entire household. From that moment Boonder became one of its recognized members, and privileges, often denied the most intelligent and valuable of his species, were quietly taken by him and submitted to by us. Thus, if he were found coiled up in a clothes-basket, or any article of clothing assumed locomotion on its own account, we only said, "O, it's Boonder," with a feeling of relief that it was nothing worse.

I have spoken of his fondness for bone-burying. It could not be called an economical faculty, for he invariably forgot the locality of his treasure, and covered the garden with purposeless holes; but although the violets and daisies were not improved by Boonder's gardening, no one ever thought of punishing him. He became a synonym for Fate; a Boonder to be grumbled at, to be accepted philosophically,—but never to be averted. But although he was not an intelligent dog, nor an ornamental dog, he possessed some gentlemanly instincts. When he performed his only feat,—begging upon his hindlegs (and looking remarkably like a penguin),—ignorant strangers would offer him crackers or cake, which he didn't like, as a reward of merit. Boonder always made a great show of accepting the proffered dainties, and even made hypocritical contortions as if swallowing, but always deposited the morsel when he was unobserved in the first convenient receptacle,—usually the visitor's overshoes.

In matters that did not involve courtesy, Boonder was sincere in his likes and dislikes. He was instinctively opposed to the railroad. When the track was laid through our street, Boonder maintained a defiant attitude toward every rail as it went down, and resisted the cars shortly after to the fullest extent of his lungs. I have a vivid recollection of seeing him, on the day of the trial trip, come down the street in front of the car, barking himself out of all shape, and thrown back several feet by the recoil of each bark.... Boonder had previously resisted the gas, but although he spent one whole day in angry altercation with the workmen,—leaving his bones unburied and bleaching in the sun,—somehow the gas went in. The Spring Valley water was likewise unsuccessfully opposed, and the grading of an adjoining lot was for a long time a personal matter between Boonder and the contractor.

These peculiarities seemed to evince some decided character and embody some idea. A prolonged debate in the family upon this topic resulted in an addition to his name,—we called him "Boonder the Conservative," with a faint acknowledgment of his fateful power. But, although Boonder had his own way, his path was not entirely of roses. Thorns sometimes pricked his sensibilities. When certain minor chords were struck on the piano, Boonder was always painfully affected and howled a remonstrance. If he were removed for company's sake to the back yard, at the recurrence of the provocation, he would go his whole length (which was something) to improvise a howl that should reach the performer. But we got accustomed to Boonder, and as we were fond of music the playing went on.

First Ladies

When an American President begins his term of office, his wife automatically becomes the First Lady. This means she is in charge of all the social activities that take place in the White House: the State dinners, balls, receptions for foreign dignitaries, and so on. It also means that she has much less time to devote to family life than other wives.

It is a challenge that has frightened some prospective First Ladies. President Franklin Pierce's wife, Jane, was reported to have fainted when her husband won his political party's nomination. And Sarah Polk was said to have prayed for her husband's defeat in the election campaign. But when the time came, when they became First Ladies, all of these women brought to the White House their own brand of courage, intelligence, and integrity.

There have been more than 40 First Ladies in the 200-plus years of America's history. Two of them were remarkably similar in their backgrounds, in the way they helped their husbands, and in the democratic ideas that they worked to make part of our country—and they lived more than 130 years apart when they served as First Ladies!

Abigail Smith was brought up on a farm in Massachusetts in the 1700's. A frail child who was considered plain, she was not sent to school, but was educated at home. She was a bright but lonely little girl. Her health eventually improved as did her social life. She fell in love with and married John Adams, a lawyer, who was deeply involved in the movement that led to the Revolutionary War and our freedom from Great Britain.

John Adams was able to pursue his career because Abigail was willing to run the family farm and raise and educate their children while he was absent during the struggle for independence. During that time hostile Indians roamed the woods around Abigail's home, disease imperiled her

and her children, and there were times during those ten years when
British troops threatened her very doorstep. But in her letters to John, she
said her hardest fight was the battle against loneliness, for she missed her
"Dearest Friend" desperately.

The Roosevelts were an aristocratic and socially prominent New York
family in the 1900's. Eleanor Roosevelt, who was awkward and not
attractive, was considered "the ugly duckling" of the family. She was
painfully shy and self-conscious, wanted no part of society, and was most
comfortable with her father. Her early training, like Abigail's, was left to
her grandmother. Education abroad, a dedicated tutor, and hard work on
her part finally brought Eleanor out of her lonely little world. Much to
everyone's surprise, she became engaged to the handsome and elegant
Franklin Roosevelt, a distant cousin.

When Franklin was crippled with infantile paralysis, Eleanor became
his "eyes" and "ears." Unlike Abigail, who stayed home while her
husband worked out his career, Eleanor traveled the world in peacetime
and wartime as Franklin's representative. In one year she traveled over
43,000 miles. Still, she was in charge of the White House, both mother
and father to the children, and hostess to the President's guests, be they
visiting royalty, government heads, or lesser government officials.

What is astonishing about these two First Ladies is that they saw shortcomings in this "land of the free and the home of the brave" and spoke out long before these conditions were corrected. In 1776 Abigail wrote to John while he and other American Patriots were composing the Declaration of Independence: ".... in the code of laws which I suppose it will be necessary for you to make, I desire you would remember the ladies and be more generous and favorable to them than your ancestors were... we will not hold ourselves bound by any law in which we have no voice or representation."

Later, almost a century before the Civil War freed the slaves, she wrote, "I wish most sincerely there were not a slave in the province. It always seemed a most iniquitous scheme to me to fight ourselves for what we are robbing the Negroes of, who have as good a right to freedom as we do."

Though slavery was no longer an issue when Eleanor Roosevelt became the First Lady, and though women had secured the right to vote, she championed social justice in this country and peace and understanding throughout the world. She did note in her writings, "One thing that I've been able to do through my work... is to help all other women to go on having more and more representation in government and world affairs." What Eleanor helped start—150 years after Abigail Adams first presented similar ideas to her husband, at a time when women could not even vote— has resulted in more equality for women in wage scales, workers' rights, and domestic equality.

Americans to Remember

Edwin **Aldrin** and Neil **Armstrong**, astronauts on the moon; Susan B. **Anthony**, suffragist.

P. T. **Barnum**, showman, for the circus; Clara **Barton**, nurse, for the Red Cross; Alexander Graham **Bell**, inventor, for the telephone.

Andrew **Carnegie**, industrialist and philanthropist; George Washington **Carver**, botanist, for the many uses of the peanut; **Chochis**, Apache chief.

Virginia **Dare**, first child of English parents born in the New World; Walt **Disney**, film maker, for Mickey Mouse and friends.

Amelia **Earhart**, aviator; Thomas Alva **Edison**, inventor, for the incandescent lamp; Albert **Einstein**, physicist.

Peggy **Fleming**, ice skater; Henry **Ford**, automaker; Robert **Fulton**, inventor, for the steamboat.

George and Ira **Gershwin**, brothers, composers; Martha **Graham**, choreographer, for modern dance.

Oliver W. **Holmes**, writer father and Supreme Court Justice son; Elias **Howe**, inventor, for the sewing machine; Julia **Howe**, writer and social reformer.

Ike (Dwight D. Eisenhower), general and President; James **Ives** (with Nathaniel Currier), lithographer, for many beautiful prints.

Andrew **Jackson** ("Old Hickory"), general and President; Thomas ("Stonewall") **Jackson**, general; Barbara **Jordan**, former congresswoman.

Helen **Keller**, author; John F. **Kennedy**, President; Francis Scott **Key**, lawyer and poet, for "The Star Spangled Banner."

Meriwether **Lewis** (with George Clark), explorer; Charles **Lindbergh**, aviator; Jack **London**, writer, for *The Call of the Wild.*

Arthur and Douglas **MacArthur**, generals, the only father and son to receive Congressional Medals of Honor; Grandma **Moses**, painter.

Carry A. **Nation**, temperance leader; Isamu **Noguchi**, sculptor and theatrical set designer.

Annie **Oakley**, sharpshooter with Buffalo Bill's Wild West Show; Jesse **Owens**, athlete, for winning four gold medals in the 1936 Olympics in Berlin.

I. M. **Pei**, architect; William **Penn**, English Quaker and founder of Pennsylvania; Matthew **Perry**, commodore, for opening Japanese ports.

Quanah, Comanche chief; James E. **Quigley**, Catholic prelate and trade union advocate.

Jackie **Robinson**, baseball player; John A. and Washington A. **Roebling**, father and son, engineers, for New York's Brooklyn Bridge; Will **Rogers**, humorist.

Issac Bashevis **Singer**, writer and Nobel prize winner; Harriet Beecher **Stowe**, writer, for *Uncle Tom's Cabin*.

Henry David **Thoreau**, naturalist and writer; Jim **Thorpe**, athlete; Harriet **Tubman**, abolitionist.

John H. **Updike**, writer; Harold C. **Urey**, chemist and Nobel prize winner.

Cornelius **Vanderbilt**, railroad and steamship industrialist; Carl and Mark **Van Doren**, brothers, writer and poet and Pulitzer prize winners.

Laura I. **Wilder**, writer; Frank Lloyd **Wright**, architect; Orville and Wilbur **Wright**, brothers, inventors of the airplane; Richard **Wright**, writer.

Malcolm **X**, writer and black leader.

Yellow Hair (George A. Custer), U.S. Army officer; Brigham **Young**, Mormon leader.

Mildred "Babe" Didrikson **Zaharias**, athlete; Florenz **Ziegfeld**, theatrical producer.

I Hear America Singing
by Walt Whitman

I hear America singing, the varied carols I hear;
Those of mechanics—each one singing his,
    as it should be, blithe and strong;
The carpenter singing his, as he measures his plank or beam,
The mason singing his, as he makes ready for work,
    or leaves off work;
The boatman singing what belongs to him in his boat—
    the deckhand singing on the steamboat deck;
The shoemaker singing as he sits on his bench—
    the hatter singing as he stands;
The wood-cutter's song—the ploughboy's, on his way in
    the morning, or at the noon intermission, or at sundown;
The delicious singing of the mother—or of the young
    wife at work—or of the girl sewing or washing—
    Each singing what belongs to her, and to none else;
The day what belongs to the day— At night, the party of
    young fellows, robust, friendly,
Singing, with open mouths, their strong melodious songs.

"Walk With Me Into a New Dignity"

In 1956 a young black minister challenged the black citizens of Montgomery, Alabama, to "Put on your walking shoes. Walk with me into a new dignity." The minister, Martin Luther King, Jr., had begun his crusade to end injustice to blacks with a bus boycott in 1955. He organized sit-ins at places where blacks were not allowed, and by 1960 over 3,000 nonviolent sit-in demonstrators had been arrested. In 1963 over 250,000 black and white Americans marched in Washington, D.C., in support of equal rights. During the march, Dr. King gave one of the most stirring speeches in American history. He shared a dream: "I have a dream that my four little children will one day live in a nation where they will not be judged by the color of their skin, but by the content of their character."

Dr. King had many experiences during his short life—from spending time in jail to conferring with the President. His life was ended by an assassin's bullet, but many shared his dreams and continue to walk with his spirit in search of a new dignity.

Another legacy of the civil rights movement is the song that has become the unquestioned anthem of all freedom movements:

> *We shall overcome, we shall overcome,*
> *We shall overcome someday.*
> *Oh, deep in my heart, I do believe,*
> *We shall overcome someday.*

The Eagle Has Landed

At 4:17 P.M. EDT on Sunday, July 20, 1969, a man was about to walk on the moon.

American astronaut Neil A. Armstrong informed NASA, "Houston, Tranquility Base, here. The Eagle has landed." While Edwin E. Aldrin, Jr., waited his turn, Armstrong descended to the moon's surface. Above, Mike Collins was alone in Columbia, patiently orbiting the moon.

From the sound of their almost casual conversation, you would hardly think that anything at all spectacular had happened.

HOUSTON: Roger, Tranquility. We copy you on the ground. You've got a bunch of guys about to turn blue. We're breathing again. Thanks a lot. (*As he made his way down the ladder to the surface, Armstrong released the automatic TV camera.*)

HOUSTON: We're getting a picture...

ARMSTRONG: I'm at the foot of the ladder...I'm going to step off...now. That's one small step for man. One giant leap for mankind. The surface is fine and powdery. I can pick it up loosely with my toe. It does adhere in fine layers like powdered charcoal to the sole and sides of my boots.

ALDRIN: It looks beautiful from here.

ARMSTRONG: It has a stark beauty all of its own. It's like much of the high desert of the United States.

ALDRIN (*leaving the LM to join Armstrong on the moon*): Okay, I'm on the top step, and I can look down over the landing-gear pads. It's a very simple matter to hop down from one step to the next.

ARMSTRONG: Yes, I found it to be very comfortable, and walking is also very comfortable. You've got three more steps and a long one.

ALDRIN: Beautiful, beautiful.

ARMSTRONG: Isn't that something? Magnificent sight down here.

ALDRIN: You got to be careful that you are leaning in the direction you want to go. In other words, you have to cross your foot over to stay underneath where your center of mass is. . . . It takes about two or three paces to make sure you've got your feet underneath you. A kangaroo hop does work, but it seems that your forward ability is not quite as good. Neil—didn't I say we might see some purple rocks?

ARMSTRONG: Find the purple rocks?

ALDRIN: Yes. They are small, sparkly.

HOUSTON (*to Mike Collins in* Columbia): *Columbia.* This is Houston reading you loud and clear. Over.

COLLINS: Yes. This is history. How's it going?

HOUSTON: . . . going beautifully. I believe they are setting up the flag now . . . you're about the only person around that doesn't have TV coverage of the scene.

COLLINS: That's right. That's all right. I don't mind a bit. How's the quality of the TV.

HOUSTON: It's beautiful, Mike. Really is. They've got the flag up, and you can see the Stars and Stripes on the lunar surface.

America the Beautiful

Katherine Lee Bates
Not too fast

Melody by Samuel A. Ward

Arranged by Norman Lloyd

O beau-ti-ful for spa-cious skies, For am-ber waves of grain,

For pur-ple moun-tain maj-es-ties A-bove the fruit-ed plain.

A-mer-i-ca! A-mer-i-ca! God shed His grace on thee,

And crown thy good with broth-er-hood From sea to shin-ing sea.

94